I'll Have to Ask my Mom

A Radio Journey

by

Warren Garling

For the three great ladies in my life,
my mom, my wife and my granddaughter

Chapter
"One" by Three Dog Night (1969)

Most of what follows is true.

Those words appear on the screen after the opening credits of my favorite movie, "Butch Cassidy and the Sundance Kid." It's the first movie I ever paid to see three times when it was on the big screen in 1969. I was a teenager at the time. After watching it on TV recently for the umpteenth time, I thought I'd borrow that line for the opening of this story.

I'm hoping this will be the riveting tale of my journey into radio as a teenager. But then again, I was hoping to be living a retired life in Maui by now. Does this den look like Maui to you? My path into radio was quite memorable (to my mother and me, anyway) and I'll attempt to share these memories in an enlightening way now that I'm retired and have finished cleaning our basement so you can actually see some of the floor, which was nearly impossible to do when I was working a full time job. But there's just so much time you can spend in the basement without starting to smell like the basement. I know this because a basement is where my first radio station was when I was about 13 years old. (How's that for a segue? I learned how to do that in radio).

Let's start in the 1960s. You remember the 60s...it was in all the newspapers. Of course, many say if you actually remember the 60s, you weren't really living them. So hop into the Wayback Machine with Mr. Peabody, Sherman and me, and meet us in 1963, when Rocky and Bullwinkle were our heroes, and I was just a very skinny 11-year-old sixth grader at Walden Elementary School in downstate New York. Well, it's downstate if you come from Schenectady, NY, like I did. Folks living in New York City call Walden "upstate." Those of us from Schenectady know where upstate really is. It's right near where the New York State legislature passes all the laws that give downstaters more money than upstaters. But that's not what I called to talk to you about, as my wife likes to say.

In 1963 we were living in a mobile home park a couple of miles east of Walden in a 10 by 60 foot trailer, my three younger brothers, one sister and I, along with mom and dad, of course. That's right, seven of us in a space so small we had to go outside to change our minds. Dad's job working on the construction of the first Beacon-Newburgh bridge brought us there from the Capital District of New York State, where we were all born. As you can imagine, I looked for any excuse to get out of the confines of our home on wheels, away from pesky siblings and out into the bigger world I was already witnessing through our black and white television and my tiny transistor radio made in Japan.

Right around the time I saw my first live murder on TV (the shooting of Lee Harvey Oswald by Jack Ruby the weekend of the Kennedy assassination), our neighbor asked my parents if they thought I'd be interested in visiting the local radio station where he hosted a 15-minute Saturday morning broadcast for the United States Air Force. You remember the Air Force. It was in all the newspapers. Harry Haines was a recruiter who used his weekly broadcast to interest young men and women to enlist in the Air Force in the early days of the Vietnam conflict.

Of course, I'm looking at all this in the rear view mirror with much older eyes that were way too young at the time to know or care where Vietnam even was. Harry could be reading chocolate cake recipes on the radio and I would have gone. The real attraction of Harry's offer was a morning out of the house, a trip across the river on the soon-to-be-outdated Beacon-Newburgh Ferry, and to get a peek at where all that music I heard on my aqua-colored two-transistor radio with telescoping antenna came from. I was enamored by the fresh Top 40 music and exciting disk jockeys I would listen to with my radio under my pillow as I fell asleep each night. (The trick, of course, was to remember to turn the radio off before actually drifting off to sleep, so that I didn't have to beg mom and dad for 69 cents for another nine volt battery every other day).

I don't remember many details about my first trip to the studios of WBNR in Beacon, NY, just across the Hudson from Newburgh, because I was suffering from a very painful toothache that morning. But as most first-time visitors to a radio station will tell you, the actual studio is a lot smaller than you imagine. And when you're 11 years old, you imagine the place from which this magical music emanates to be a grand palace, a stage with a cavernous room for an audience. Uh-uh. I remember one small studio, with room for maybe three people, if one of them is as skinny as I was.

Recognizing my toothache pain that morning, Harry invited me to join him again a few weeks later, and this is when I decided I no longer wanted to be Roy Rogers when I grew up. Now I wanted to be on the radio. An announcer—a DJ! Looking back, I believe as an 11-year-old I was quite taken by the lights and the bouncing meters on the control board and equipment rack, and all that the DJ had control of, including three huge record players I later learned were called turntables. Because the studio itself wasn't anything to write home about, and while our host DJ was pleasant enough, he was too busy to share too many details about his life in radio. I wonder if he had told me about how the radio business doesn't pay most disk jockeys very well, if I would have thought differently about pursuing a career in such an addictive vocation. Probably not. I was immediately hooked.

Weeks after my second visit, the music I was enjoying on the New York City radio stations I could pick up on my battery-eating transistor radio changed dramatically. With the arrival of the Beatles in America in early 1964, I was more convinced than ever that I needed to play this music on the radio myself. While I was just beginning to pay more attention to the terrifically talented DJs on New York City radio stations like WABC and WMCA, I would play my Swan Records 45 rpm copy of "She Loves You" backed with "I'll Get You" over and over again, pretending to introduce the song to my vast radio audience of three brothers and a sister in our cramped 10 by 10 foot bedroom which slept four (the youngest not quite 2 years old and still sleeping in a crib).

By the way, about that Swan Records copy of "She Loves You." I'd love to tell you I still owned that historic, quite valuable piece of vinyl, but I learned the hard way one day in the late 60s that leaving a record on the back shelf of your mom's Ford Galaxy automobile on a hot summer's day is a great way to turn your prized possession into a warped, useless piece of black plastic that resembled an ashtray with a hole in the middle. I cried that day...and again just now recounting my loss.

I don't remember many of the DJs names from this time, except "Cousin Brucie," whom, interestingly, I would cross paths with some 30 years later. Remind me to tell you that story in a future chapter.

You know what? Let's do it now, since I know you'll forget to remind me and I'll forget I told you to remember to remind me...or something like that. The year is 1989, and I'm now working part-time in radio on one of the stations I grew up listening to, 980/WTRY in Troy, NY, known in the 60s and early 70s as "The Great 98!" The station was now an "oldies" station, playing the hits from its heyday. I was working Saturday mornings from 6 to 10, while working full-time in professional services marketing. I was also a volunteer on the local PBS-TV station, WMHT, occasionally appearing on live TV during membership drives to raise money for the non-profit. As it happens, WTRY and WMHT were teaming up one Friday evening to air a prerecorded television program of 60s rock n' roll artists that was hosted by none other than the aforementioned "Cousin" Bruce Morrow of New York City radio fame.

"The Cuz" came to town to appear on WTRY to promote the Friday night airing of his special on WMHT, and I had been chosen to co-host the TV broadcast with him that evening. Needless to say, I was a bowl of Jell-O at the prospect of meeting and working with a man whose voice was one of my early influences as a preteen. Brucie was as nice as could be, and easy to work with in front of the TV cameras, while we "begged for dollars," as my wife always called it. We spent the better part of that Friday evening asking viewers to become members of Public Television during breaks in the programming.

But the real kicker came the next morning when, after about four hours of sleep, I was live on the radio playing the greatest oldies of all time, and talking about what fun we'd had the night before on TV with Brucie. About a half-hour into my shift I got a call on the studio phone from my radio idol, who had taken a moment before leaving for the airport to call and tell me, "Ya' sound great, kid!" Now, this man didn't have to do that. Call me "kid." I was almost 40 years old. That gives you some idea of the kind of guy he is. And it also tells you that either he wasn't fully awake after our work the previous evening, or that I should have been seeking work in a larger radio market.

I shared the news of that call with my audience a few minutes later and declared that I could retire now, completely fulfilled. To have a legendary radio entertainer like Bruce Morrow tell you he liked what he heard, was the ultimate prize in a business that changes air talent more frequently than I change my socks. No amount of money, no amount of audience, no amount of years behind the microphone could top that feeling. It's why I still do what I do, even for just a few hours a week.

Chapter
"Two Divided by Love" by The Grass Roots (1971)

But I digress. (Is there something I could take to keep that from happening?) What was I talking about before I so rudely interrupted myself? Oh yeah, the music! Ah…the music of 1964. One of the best years for rock n' roll by far. Songs written and recorded just for the preteen me, by some artists not much older than me. How could I not beg my mom and dad to turn it on when we were in the car together? Beg all I want, dad would have none of it. A few years later Mom would acquiesce when dad wasn't in the car. But dad's idea of good highway music was instrumental versions of hit songs played on what I later learned were called middle-of-the-road or M-O-R stations. Don't look for any of these on your iHeartRadio app, you won't find them. While mom would be nice enough to buy us the occasional Beatles single at Christmas or on birthdays, dad would be the one yelling "turn that music down!" when we got a bit too generous with the volume. But you'll grow to appreciate him like I did for other important reasons later in the story.

Soon after the Fab Four arrived in the United States dad changed jobs, which moved us back to the Capital District of New York, East Glenville, to be exact. I know, you've never heard of such a place, but the suburb of Schenectady was big enough to have not only a Glenville but a West Glenville, to boot. So there! This move put us in an actual house for the first time. No wheels underneath. This proved very advantageous when my desire to be on the radio resulted in the construction of my own basement pirate radio station. By pirate I don't mean "Arg, maties!" But rather a station not authorized to broadcast by the Federal Communications Commission. I believe somewhere it's written that every teenager hoping to break into radio during the Top 40 era had to have their own basement or bedroom radio station. I learned later quite a few colleagues prepared for their careers this way.

We didn't necessarily need a large audience, it was just our way of imitating the guys on the radio (and they were mostly guys, back then), and pretending that someday we'd actually have more than just our siblings and parents listening on the upstairs kitchen radio, if we were lucky and talented enough. A few years back I read about the "10,000 hour rule." It states that after about 10,000 hours of working at a chosen profession or practicing to get good at something, you were considered an expert, or at least really proficient at your chosen vocation. The author cited The Beatles as a perfect example of that. Before they had their worldwide success, they had worked on stage together for more than 6 years. Talk about honing your craft.

So I determined that to get good at DJ'ing, I would need to have my own radio station for practice. No one suggested this to me and I don't remember seeing anything written in a book or magazine or aired on TV that would suggest this was a good idea. Somehow I was being led in a direction that I just knew was the right one. I suppose it would be the same as deciding that if I wanted to play baseball like Mickey Mantle, I would have to practice playing baseball. I do remember that I was never discouraged by either of my parents in my pursuit. They even bought me kits suitable for my age that taught me how to build a working radio to listen to and one that would actually wirelessly broadcast your voice through a radio.

Now, I've never been very good at building things, you can ask my wife. And some of the experiments I tried didn't work. I only thank my parents for not buying me a chemistry set.

My first radio station was in a finished basement paneled in the then-popular genuine knotty pine with linoleum-tiled floor. Our basement was large enough for a couple of beds, a TV sitting area complete with couch and chairs, and even a pool table. One end of the room featured a built-in desk probably six to eight feet long, complete with built-in bookshelves, which I quickly commandeered as the perfect spot for WSCG Radio, named for **W**arren-**S**cott-and **C**raig-**G**arling. Not that I'd ever let my two next-oldest brothers actually play with my radio equipment. And by radio equipment I mean a homemade control panel or "board" (again, that radio parlance). Mine was actually constructed from a board, a length of plywood that I drilled holes into, to hold too loud, cheap toggle switches I bought at the pre-Radio Shack local Lafayette Electronics store in downtown Schenectady, and a 45 rpm record player I opened up and hard wired into the quarter-watt radio transmitter my folks bought me for Christmas.

The record player was an automatic record changer, so my early broadcasts to the kitchen upstairs (that's as far as a quarter-watt of broadcast power with an indoor antenna will get ya') featured me talking at the end of one song while the next record dropped down to the turntable to be played. You learn pretty quick to be short, succinct and sharp with the wit, as it was difficult to cleanly stop or delay this sophisticated automation.

Eventually I was able to add a small 3" reel-to-reel tape recorder to the set up, which allowed me a bit more time to get the next "hit" ready to play. The tape recordings I made and played were often of new songs I recorded with a cheap microphone off our TV set, especially on Saturday afternoons when Dick Clark would bring *American Bandstand* to the teenagers of America. I mean, come on! Hit singles cost 69 cents at the local Woolworth's record bins, money that was hard-earned by delivering the Scotia-Glenville Journal, a free weekly newspaper, for a penny a copy. My $1.37 a week salary didn't buy me many singles. That's why, when my brother Scott bought the occasional 45 with his allowance, I would add it to the station's music library, much to his chagrin.

I whiled away the hours after school and sometimes complete days on the weekends and during summer breaks, practicing (read: copying) the sound of the local Top 40 DJs. What I wouldn't give to have the log I kept of the hours spent behind that tin microphone broadcasting all the way upstairs to the kitchen. I'm afraid it didn't survive the years after I left the basement for college. But I don't want to get ahead of myself. I'm just 12 going on 13 years old at this juncture, spending so much time in the basement that my mother would almost have to drag me outside by my crew cut to see any sunshine. I really didn't want to play outside. I was having way too much fun by myself in the basement. At one point I remember we compromised, and I took my radio equipment "mobile" to my neighbor's backyard for my first outdoor remote broadcast. Note: when you take records in the hot sunshine, it's a good idea to play them in the shade, as the sun can do a real number on the viability of the vinyl. See the "She Loves You" parable, above.

At one point in these practice years my mother came home from grocery shopping one day to hear music coming from the table radio on the kitchen counter. She listened as the announcer told his audience what they had just heard and what song was now starting to play. She stopped in her tracks and said to herself, "That sounds like Warren on the radio." And, of course, it was. She yelled down the stairs to see if she was actually listening to WSCG, and I assured her it was me. When she told me I sounded like the "real thing", I knew I had arrived or was at least on the right track. And I had my first fan, despite the fact she wasn't in the demographic of the audience I was seeking.

Chapter
"Three Coins in the Fountain" by The Four Aces (1955)

Soon enough, life brought me to the 9th grade at Burnt Hills-Ballston Lake Junior High School, where my guidance counselor, Mr. Carow, told me about a local radio station that had an after-school internship program where you could help out around their studios for a couple of hours once a week. This excited me to no end, and I still think of Mr. Carow quite fondly for sending me in this direction. Without the encouragement of adults like him and my parents, I'm sure I'd be asking to this day "You want fries with that?"

WSNY in Schenectady was a 1,000-watt daytime/250-watt nighttime "easy listening" formatted radio station at 1240 on the AM dial. This meant that they played the quieter hit recording artists of the day. Crooners, mostly, like Dean Martin, Frank Sinatra, Vic Damone, and probably some female artists of the day that I don't remember hearing. But it wasn't the format that drew me to these pretty much hole-in-the-wall studios on Lafayette Street in the city that was home to the General Electric Company. It was the prospect of learning about my hopefully future profession from the inside.

Never mind that most of my Friday afternoons were spent cutting out ads from the Schenectady Gazette newspaper, or getting coffee for the air personalities (real DJs you could listen to in the car on the way to and from the station!). I was at the center of the universe of where I wanted to spend the rest of my working life. Sort of. A small local station was not the dream of where one wanted to end up as much as a starting point for bigger stations and bigger cities. But it was a start. And it's where most eventually successful air personalities got their start. The training ground, if you will.

So every Friday afternoon after school in the spring of 1967 mom would load up all six of us kids into the family tank and drop off her oldest at the radio station for a couple of hours. Luckily, dad worked at the time as a car salesman at a nearby Ford dealership, so he could pick me up on his dinner break to get me home. Not that I really ever wanted to leave. I would have lived at the station, if that were allowed. Besides the meaningless gofer duties, I was being taught how to operate the equipment in the production studio, where I eventually was trained to dub commercials and public service announcements from reel-to-reel recording tape to tape cartridges called "carts" in radio vernacular. How can I explain to you the feeling I had when I would hear a commercial I dubbed actually played on the radio? Remember how you felt when you saw Neil Armstrong walk on the moon for the first time? It was like that. Only with more gravity.

At the end of my 9th grade year at BH-BL, I was expected to stop going to the station on Friday afternoons. But I didn't. I couldn't. And no one really told me I HAD to. When many years later I ran into another junior high intern I volunteered with at the time, and I told him I didn't stop at the end of the school year, he said to me, "Why didn't I think of that?" He, too, went to the same broadcasting college I went to and into a brief career in radio.

So throughout the summer mom would make sure I got there around 3 every Friday afternoon, and dad would usually remember to pick me up on the way home for dinner. This continued into the beginning of my tenth grade year of high school, when 1240/WSNY changed music formats and became the Top 40 home of "The Young

Americans!" Gone were the Ray Conniff Singers offering their adult version of "In-a-Gadda-Da-Vida" for the actual hit record by Iron Butterfly! But also gone was the last remaining after school intern. With new professionals came the edict that "kids couldn't be hanging around the station getting in the way." So I was asked to stop appearing on their doorstep every Friday after school. I was crushed. Career over, before it began.

However, this minor set-back didn't stop me from keeping in touch with some of these new air personalities that were now playing real music on the station. I quickly made friends with the evening personality who went by the name of Tom Jefferson on the air. His real name was Roger Anthony Del Nero, Jr., if you were to believe the name on his third class FCC license hanging on the studio wall. But with the "Young American" sound of this new Top 40 outlet came disk jockey's using names like Paul Revere, George Washington, John Tyler and my friend Thomas "Tom" Jefferson. I'm not sure who came up with the "Young Americans" theme, but I know it was meant to compete locally with the "Lively Ones" on WTRY in Troy and "The Good Guys" of WPTR in Albany.

For a time, to set the station apart from any other you might think you were listening to (because we all played the same Top 40 songs), whenever you heard a "Young American" talking between the songs, you heard fife and drum music playing quietly just underneath the announcer's voice. This not only helped make the station's sound unique, but also kept the air personalities from speaking into the beginning of the next hit song as it began to play, a common practice of the day called the "talk up." A good DJ would know just how to say what needed to be said and end his complete thought just as the lyrics of the song started. That's called "hitting the post." But with music already playing under the talking DJ, they couldn't talk up any songs.

Isn't that interesting? Think of all the technical stuff I'm teaching you here. With practice, you too, could be a 1960s DJ on the radio. Just send $19.95, cash, check or money order (no stamps, please) to...

Chapter
"**Four** Strong Winds" by Ian and Sylvia (1963)

So back to the story. Tom and I spoke on the phone almost nightly. I would call him just to shoot the breeze while taking a break from not understanding my algebra homework, and constantly remind him that one day I was going to be a radio DJ just like him. I thought it was part of his job description as an air personality I had chosen to listen to and call on the phone, to talk to me when I called. It wasn't until I entered radio myself that I found this to be a bit distracting at times. I mean, think about it. How would you like your surgeon to take a phone call from a future surgeon and talk to him while cradling the phone on his shoulder and repairing your spleen?

But as an avid fan, I didn't think I was bothering the guy. And Tom was always very encouraging and never talked down to me. The same with the other DJs I was listening to on competing area Top 40 radio stations. Often I would be the correct caller to win a hit single or album, and before I could even tell the "jock" who I was, he would say, "Congratulations, Warren!" Wow, he remembered my voice! That's got to mean something, right?

Months went by while I listened to a couple of other BH-BL students make their way on to the local radio airwaves. Bob Hall was two years older than I, and as a senior in high school became an on-air traffic reporter doing live reports from the WTRY traffic helicopter afternoons after school. How cool is that? He got to be on the radio AND fly in a helicopter at the same time! And high school junior Jim LeLevre (known on the air as Jim Leonard) began doing part-time work in nearby Saratoga Springs on WKAJ AM & FM. I was so jealous, and used to tell them so. But I figured if they could do it, why couldn't I?

For a time in about 1967 or '68, I was excited to be chosen a "High School Hot Line" reporter for the 50,000-watt powerhouse Top 40 giant WPTR at 1540 AM in Albany. This consisted of a weekly one-minute report I would phone in to the station announcing the top 3 hit songs as voted on by the students at BH-BL High School, or at least the students I could corner in the hallways between classes. I was also allowed to then talk about something going on at the high school, like the school play or our next football game. I was slowly becoming known in school as that bothersome kid always asking "What's your favorite song on the radio this week?" But it paid off, as I got some brief exposure on a real radio station, and learned how to sound professional in my presentation over the phone. Looking back, I now realize I could truthfully tell people I made my radio debut on a 50,000 radio station at the age of 15! NOW I think of it.

It was about this time that our school principal, Mr. Sewell, walked into my study hall one day toward the end of my sophomore year, and scared the pants off me. I was never in trouble in school, a real goody-two-shoes, as we used to be known. I had never even spoken to the principle, and here he was coming into my study hall and asking to see me! My study hall classmates starting murmuring "Uh-oh" and "Oooo, you're in trouble now." They obviously didn't know me well. It turns out he wanted to let me know I had been recommended to be the co-host of the morning announcement program on the school's public address system, starting in the fall. He asked if I would be interested in co-hosting with Wesley Smith, the student council president and future senior class clown (no, they're not mutually exclusive). Yes, another step in the right direction for my budding career as an announcer. Can't you just sense it coming?

"The Wes and Warren Show" debuted in September 1968. I didn't care about billing. Wes was a senior, I was a junior, and he was a lot better known in school than I was. And we were an immediate hit. I mean, come on, everyone in the school listened! Of course, they didn't have a choice, but that's beside the point. I now had an immediate fan base of almost a thousand people, if you included the teachers and janitors. Well, "fan base" might be a stretch, but you can't beat the recognition factor. Wes and I would make the morning announcements and add a little humorous (we hoped) patter on occasion. Those daily five to ten minutes gave me a forum and foundation for my future career in radio. And Wes used this as a training ground for his future career...as a Methodist minister. Hey, we each have our own calling. God bless.

Notoriety in high school, however, can work both ways. With my new found popularity I was even more talkative in class. And one day when caught whispering to a friend of mine in gym class while Coach Plimpton was trying to explain the finer points of how to throw a dodge ball, I heard the loud admonishment, "Garling, if you don't shut up I'm going to shove that microphone down your throat!" Hey, even the coach was a fan.

Of course, at home during my junior year of high school, I was still practicing my DJ shtick on my basement radio station, re-named WSCO (short for Scotia, our mailing address). I thought this might help keep my brothers at bay and away from my equipment, since the station was no longer named after them. At the same time I was studying to take my FCC Third Class (with Element 9 endorsement) License exam. In order to work on the radio at the time, you had to have at least a Third Class license with a special element to allow you to take transmitter meter readings. This was supposed to keep the riff-raff off the radio, but anyone that listened to local 1960s Top 40 radio knows *that* didn't work.

I had to take the test twice, as I failed one of the three elements the first time. Not the hardest element that dealt with the technical transmitter reading stuff, but an easier element that tripped me up because THIS WAS A TEST! I hated tests (still do) and always had trouble with them in school. I know you've heard this excuse from "D" students before, but I was a "B" or at least "C+" student during most of my high school education. I just froze up on exams, like I proceeded to do at the United States Post Office in Schenectady, where they offered the FCC exam a couple of times a year.

But once I had that 5 x 7 inch government-issued light blue-colored license in my possession, I was ready to take on the world, or at least the local radio stations. Only one more thing stood in my way, if you don't count not having a drivers' license to get to any job, should I land one. I needed an audition tape, what's called an "aircheck" in the industry. This consisted of a recording of the announcer's voice between records and into commercial breaks. You don't include the whole songs, just your announcing into and out of them. Luckily, I had a place to record such a thing: my basement radio station. So that's what I did. I don't remember how many takes I did, but I know it was a true "aircheck" because I didn't edit the recording in any other way. It was about five minutes of my announcer style, using pretty current hit records and a couple of commercials I'd written from newspaper ads with some added background music.

One more small step was necessary before I could start sending this 5" recorded reel of rollicking repartee to the local program directors at nearby radio stations. I needed multiple copies of the recording. Since I only owned one tape recorder, I couldn't record copies or "dubs," in radio nomenclature. So I thought I'd ask my Spanish teacher (whom I'm sure I was impressing with my mangling of a second language) if I could use the school's Language Lab facilities. She had a master machine in the front of the classroom that would play to individual desks in the classroom equipped with built-in tape recorders. I explained my dilemma to her (one of the many loyal fans of my morning announcements show), and she was very nice to say yes, I could use the room after school one afternoon. I'm sure she would have been more impressed if we had discussed this conversing in Spanish but, again, I was just a C student, at best. Comprende?

Now it's still unbelievable to me, almost 50 years later, that a grown professional radio program director wouldn't jump at the chance to hire a somewhat talented, self-taught 16-year-old high school junior with short, neatly combed hair and horn-rimmed glasses and at least three years of basement radio station experience — and let's not forget a Third Class FCC License with endorsement — to work at least part-time on their successful 5,000 or even 50,000 watt radio station. I wasn't asking for much. I'd even start with a nighttime or overnight shift! I wasn't picky.

But believe it or not, I didn't hear back from a single one of the stations in my area when I sent out my first round of tapes. Kinda disappointing. Of course I should have made some follow-up phone calls, but since I didn't do that to get my weekly newspaper delivery job, what did I know? Nevertheless, I was determined to stay on as many radars as possible as the summer between my junior and senior year of high school approached. I decided I would re-record my audition. Maybe I chose some songs my future bosses didn't like…or I didn't talk fast enough…or too fast. Then, the incredible happened.

Chapter
"Five Years" by David Bowie (1972)

The evening of my last day of the school year in 1969 was a Thursday…a Thursday that resides in my memory as if it were this morning. Now that school was out for the summer, I was starting my vacation by babysitting my two young cousins, Kimmy and Kenny (you know them as Kim and Ken, now that they're adults). They lived just a couple miles from our house, and I was probably in their kitchen looking for food when their phone rang. On the other end of the call was Tom Jefferson. Yes, the same Tom Jefferson who worked the evening shift at WSNY where I had interned starting in 9th grade.

My first question to him was, "How did you find me?"

"Well, what do you think? I called your house and your mom gave me this number," he replied. Of course, stupid, I said to myself. How else would he know where to find me? I've said stupid things like this all my life. While working in television many years later an old neighbor of mine once called me at work about speaking to a middle school class she taught, and I asked her how she found me. She said, "I saw you on TV last night." Of course, stupid, I said to myself. Way to make an impression.

So once we established how Tom found me, my mind started racing because I knew he hadn't called to see how I was doing or whether or not I could babysit for him. I didn't know anything about his personal life, only his radio persona. Then he uttered the following words, which I remember as if you asked me what I had for breakfast today:

"How'd you like to work on the radio this weekend?"

I'd like to believe my reply was something smart and funny like, "How much do I have to pay you?" But, of course, I have no recollection of my immediate reply because my head had just exploded completely off my shoulders. This is the perfect example of the words of wisdom you have no doubt heard over the years: "It's not WHAT you know, it's WHO you know." All my years of "playing radio" in my basement, singing along with my favorite songs on my favorite radio stations growing up, and bothering nighttime DJs with phone calls to those same favorite stations, and it wasn't my talent that warranted this phone call. It was because I knew Tom. But all my years of laying the groundwork were about to culminate with the beginning of my lifelong career in radio.

And I didn't get this offer by sending out an audition tape, or nervously sitting behind a microphone auditioning in a studio somewhere. I got the offer because Tom's boss had forgotten to find a fill-in for him for the pending weekend, when Tom needed to go out of town to a wedding. Time being of the essence, Tom told me he explained to his boss who I was and that he was sure that, with a few hours of training, I'd be able to handle the job. Tom's faith in me may have been stronger than my own at this point, but I wasn't going to pass up this chance. Tom's boss said, "OK, but he's your responsibility. If he screws up it's on you." No pressure.

He was asking me to work from midnight to six Friday night into Saturday morning, and then again from midnight until seven Saturday night into Sunday morning. He further explained that if I could come in Friday evening when he started his shift at 7:00, he could easily train me how to run the equipment and take the meter readings, etc. by the time the shift started at midnight.

"I'll have to ask my mom," was the only reply I could think of.

"Well, I've done that already, when I just spoke to her," he said. "She said she'd make sure you got to and from the station this weekend. Are you in?"

I replied in the affirmative I'm sure, but as I said, without my head that had just blown into bits and pieces all over my cousins' kitchen, I really don't remember my exact words. I'm sure I called my mother back and she reminded me that I was expected to attend the high school graduation of my girlfriend Robin, and the subsequent graduation party, both of them on Saturday. I said I'd make it work. Somehow.

At almost 17 years of age (this was about a month before my birthday), I had plenty of energy, and would probably be running on nerves and adrenalin all weekend anyway. To be safe, I tried to take a short nap on Friday afternoon, my first full day of summer vacation, and then mom and dad started a free taxi service that, unbeknownst to us, would last all summer. I promised my supportive girlfriend that I'd still be there for her special weekend, I just couldn't assure her I'd be awake for all of it. She understood, and said she was just as excited as I was.

In fact, it was this very girlfriend, Robin Allen, who came up with the name she thought I could use on the radio. Most professionals didn't use their real names on the air, they used "air names" that were easily understood and, hopefully, memorable. There was the added benefit that your air name wouldn't appear in the local phone book, which normally would allow excited listeners to call you at home in the middle of the night requesting you play "Sugar, Sugar" by the Archies on the radio tomorrow. The monopoly that was the phone company at that time published the only book in the world that you had to pay to keep your name *out* of.

Robin had always liked the name "Christopher Robin," from the classic children's story *Winnie the Pooh,* for obvious reasons. But she liked it not just for the connection to her given name, but the way it flowed off the tongue. She suggested "Christopher Warren" would do the same for me on the radio. I thought it was brilliant and loved it from the moment she suggested it. Of course, I was so enamored with Robin, my first steady girl, whom I'd been dating throughout my junior year of high school that I probably would have loved Joey Jones if she suggested it. Little did I realize that I wouldn't get a chance to use my chosen air name until more than a year later and that Robin wouldn't know I actually adopted it for more than a decade into my career.

Most of the Garlings in the family had no problem with me using a professional name. They understood the reasoning and the benefits. All except my grandmother. My dad's mom Edna was always disappointed that she had to explain to her friends that her radio star grandson was Chris Warren. She wanted it to be more obvious, obviously. I think she eventually got over it.

However, I was about to find the whole discussion about an air name was moot, because when I arrived at the radio station Friday evening around 7, I found out my air name had been chosen for me. Turns out lots of radio stations at the time had a given set of names that they had made into music jingles or shouts, when you hear the singers sing, for example, a name like "Jesse James!" And that's who I was about to become at midnight. It wasn't a name you'd immediately associate with the station's Young Americans theme, but I guess because of my age, it made more sense than John Adams or Ben Franklin.

I later found out I wasn't the first Jesse James on the station and probably wouldn't be the last, but for now Jesse it was, whether I liked it or not. But before the radio audience could meet the latest edition of Jesse James, I had a few hours of control board and meter reading training to undergo. Tom was very patient as he showed me all ten or twelve control knobs ("pots", short for potentiometers) on the board, each controlling the volume of the turntables, cart machines, microphones and I don't remember what else. It looks complicated to the layman, but Tom's guidance was good. He said unlike a car, where your hands, feet and eyes have to work in harmony to successfully navigate, my two hands would control just one or two pots at a time, in most instances.

"Just don't cross your hands when reaching for a pot," he explained. Pretty simple, and words that have stuck with me through all these years. I still can't chew gum and walk at the same time, but I'm a master control board operator.

Tom gave me plenty of time to absorb all this knowledge which I inhaled like my first plate of spaghetti at dinner, trying to beat out my five siblings to get a second helping. By eleven o'clock he thought I was ready to take the controls while he still did the talking. I remember it going rather smoothly, as I easily segued from a record to the announcer's microphone to commercial cart to jingle cart and back to a record. As I mentioned earlier, the Young Americans fife and drum music would play quietly in the background whenever the microphone was turned on, which meant it didn't sound good when the music intro was playing at the beginning of a record. So the jocks would introduce the song and then start playing it, turning the mic off and not talking over the beginning of the record.

At least two or three times during my practice hour I would forget to turn Tom's mic off when I started the next record. Sometimes I would start talking to him and hear myself in the headphones, which

I'm sure was an interesting experience for the listener, but not for the embarrassed virgin board operator. Tom just chuckled. Once, when I left the mic on, Tom began whistling along with the fife and drum music that was now competing with the latest Top 40 hit by Tommy James and the Shondells. I quickly turned the mic off, red faced.

But to be honest, everything else I remember from that first hour was that I did a pretty good job engineering the sound of the station. Tom said I was a natural and was really comfortable with the fact that he was about to let me open my mouth and actually begin my radio announcing career at midnight. He said if the phone rang, just ignore it until I became comfortable doing what I needed to do while the song was playing. This consisted of taking the last record off the turntable, returning it to the bottom of the correct pile of hits, picking out the next song from the next category on the format clock hanging over the control board, getting jingles and commercials lined up to play, and thinking about what I might say when the song ended and before I started the next element.

Of course I was a sixteen year-old smarty pants with his own radio show so I'm sure I took phone calls pretty close to the moment Tom left the building. He didn't leave right away. He said he'd sit in the nearby newsroom, which had a window into the main studio, and stand by in case something when horribly wrong.

So at midnight I played the short station identification or legal ID as it was called, "WSNY…Schenectady," and hit the power switch for the first song I had cued up on the turntable. Oh, yeah, you don't know about cuing up records, do you? Sorry about that. It's kind of important, to keep the show moving smoothly, that the next record start when you wanted it to. So we'd take the tone arm and place the needle near the beginning of the record and run it forward manually until we heard the sound of the song start. We did this off the air with the pot turned to down to "cue" on the board, so only we could hear it in a small speaker in the board. Then we'd back the record up a quarter to half a turn on the turntable, so when we started it, it wouldn't make a "wow" sound as it came up to speed. There are other ways to accomplish this, but that's for my next book, "The Care and Feeding of Your Turntable."

Believe it or not, I remember my first two records I played on the air on this early summer night in 1969. Neither became number one, but they're two of my favorite songs from the summer of the first man on the moon, Woodstock and the Amazin' Mets. At midnight Saturday, June 21st "What Does it Take? (To Win your Love from Me)" by Jr. Walker and the All Stars was aired on WSNY/1240 in Schenectady, NY. No one else on earth would remember this, but ask most DJs from the rock n' roll era and they could probably tell you the name of the record that started their career.

Two minutes and thirty-four seconds later (I just checked the record length on the Interweb), I segued into the next hit, "My Pledge of Love" by the Joe Jeffrey Group." What happened after that, what I played, what I said, what mistakes I made, are lost in the ether. I just know I was having the time of my life. A five year dream was finally coming true, if only for that weekend.

Much of the rest of the weekend is a blur. I don't remember much about attending Robin's graduation ceremony in nearby Saratoga Springs, nor her party that afternoon that was within walking distance of our house. But after another brief early-evening nap mom or dad again delivered me to the studios just before midnight Saturday and retrieved me at seven Sunday morning. I'm sure I slept long and deep that Sunday morning dreaming about what would happen from here. Had the program director liked what he heard? Had he even stayed up to listen?

Chapter
"**Six** Days on the Road" by Dave Dudley (1963)

I didn't have to wait too long for the answer. Program director Don DeRosa called Monday afternoon and introduced himself to me on the phone. He said not only did he like what he heard, but he wondered if I'd be interested in working the 3:00 to 7:00 PM ("afternoon drive") shift for the summer. Once I got up off the kitchen floor (and asked my mother if she and/or dad could continue the taxi service), I accepted the offer. We didn't talk money, as that was secondary to me. I had my first full-time job in broadcasting. As I've said before, I would have paid them. Little did I know at the time that disk jockey's do it for the love of the job, because very few of us in radio become rich.

While many new disk jockeys were relegated, rightfully so, to the midnight to six shift in order to hone their skills without too big an audience witnessing their on-the-air training, I was being asked to work the second most listened-to shift on weekday radio, just behind the morning drive shift in popularity. I don't remember thinking that at the time, just that I was going to get a chance to do more of what I had done over the weekend, only to a potentially much larger audience. I say potentially, because if I screwed this up and I lost the audience left listening to me by the ten to three personality, "Paul Revere," I wouldn't be working that shift, or perhaps any shift, for very long.

While I have no memory of anyone sharing any ratings information with me that summer, I assumed I was holding my own by frequent critiques from my new boss. He would often appear just after my show ended at 7:00 to share his thoughts and give me guidance. I don't remember thinking, "What is he doing here? He did the 6 to 10 morning shift, so he's been up since before dawn and he's still here at sunset." I guess if I had realized that, I might never have taken the position of program director myself about 11 years later at another station. Programming a 24-hour radio station means your responsibilities never go to bed.

Don and I got along just fine, in my memory, as he treated me quite professionally. I learned a lot from him, especially one of the most important traits of successful program directors in radio. When he heard me say something or do something on the air that needed attention or change, he didn't usually come bursting into the studio in the middle of my shift to tell me. He sought me out AFTER my shift ended, so it wouldn't affect my performance while on the air. I've heard from too many colleagues over the years that their bosses wouldn't hesitate to interrupt their creative flow by critiquing them on the spot.

Some of our more interesting (read: heated) conversations stick with me, as you'd expect from a teenager trying to learn fast on his first job and trying to please everyone at work AND listening on the radio. In fact, he actually broke his first commandment of not critiquing the talent in the middle of their shift, when he called me one Saturday afternoon to tell me to watch the flow of my music. Well, he didn't put it quite as nicely as that. I could tell he was upset. I learned a lot of new words while working for Don, none of which I'd heard at home or even in Spanish class. Sometimes I thought he was using these expletives just to see me blush, but they certainly helped him get his point across.

When you're picking the records to play, as we did during the golden age of Top 40 radio, you have to be careful not to jar the audience too much by playing a quiet Frank Sinatra ballad directly before or after the latest release from Led Zeppelin. Not smart. Listeners actually have a tendency to check to see what your competition further up the radio dial is playing when you awake them from their radio hypnosis. Like that warm, sunny summer Saturday afternoon when I finished playing a rather subdued hit by a female artist and went directly into the power opening guitar chords of "Hot Smoke & Sassafras" by a group called Bubble Puppy. Listen to it on line sometime and you'll understand what I'm talking about. This shows you how much of an impression his call made on me that day. I can remember the exact song that exacted his wrath that once-beautiful and peaceful summer afternoon.

He explained that he was at a nearby park relaxing like many others who weren't spending their summer Saturdays working, listening to our station being played on a nearby listener's transistor radio that was hanging from a tree limb. He was quite happy that these nearby Schenectadians were listening to his radio station. When I performed the direct segue from relaxing pop music to loud heavy metal, the listener quickly grabbed his radio and tuned it to another popular local station that had disk jockeys with a lot more experience and who got paid more than I did. This upset my now-harried boss to the point that he sought out the nearest pay phone and ripped me a new orifice with which I could insert the filling of my choice. So to speak. Never made that mistake again.

Another instance during my early learning process where I crossed paths with a cross boss, involved not following the format. Every station has a format, usually laid out not just by the type of music played but the order and timing of the music heard within an hour on the radio. To balance the music played throughout the day by different air personalities, we followed a "format clock." Records were categorized usually by letters, "A" records being the most popular at the time (usually the top ten or twenty hits). The "A" records were played most often in an hour. "B" records represented up and coming hits and they weren't played as often. "C" records were usually some relatively new unproven artists with records you hoped would become hits. You might hear two of these in an hour. And "D" records, usually four or five brand new releases were played just perhaps one time per shift, to give them exposure and glean the response of the listener before moving it up a category or off the radio entirely.

At WSNY/1240, the Home of the Young Americans, in August of 1969, there was a new record released by Sly and the Family Stone that was going to be a stone-cold smash. I knew it, the boss knew it, the listeners loved it. But since it was new and in the "D" category, it was introduced to our audience by being offered once every four hours during the first week of its release. Standard practice by many radio stations. That means, if you followed the format clock, and your shift was four hours long, you could only play the record once per shift.

Try telling that to a just 17-year-old future Broadcasting Hall of Fame DJ (hey, a guy can dream, can't he?) who just knew what his audience wanted. They wanted to hear "Hot Fun in the Summertime" in the 3 o'clock hour and again in the 6 o'clock hour. So that's what I did. I skipped the fourth record in that four-record rotation and played the song a second time in my shift. I mean, who would know? A good program director who always seemed to be listening, that's who. When my shift ended, Don called me into his office as I turned the opposite way down the hallway out of the studio toward the station exit.

He said to me with a big smile on his face, "You like that new Sly and the Family Stone song, eh?" I replied enthusiastically, "Yes, it's gonna be a big hit."

"Do you want to be able to still play it on your show when it gets into the top ten?"

"Sure."

"THEN DON'T EVER LET ME HEAR YOU BREAKING FORMAT AGAIN!"

Of course, he said it louder than those all-capital letters indicate. I believe this is the first time anyone outside my family ever yelled at me. If you don't count Coach Plimpton with his insertion suggestion for my microphone back in gym class. Scared the pants off me. Never made that mistake again.

Chapter
"**Seven** Wonders" by Fleetwood Mac (1987)

But besides these two instances that have stuck with me for almost 50 years, I don't remember any other attitude adjustments necessary to help me understand the inner workings of Top 40 radio broadcasting. Most of my afternoon shifts that summer were filled with light, brief chatter that only a naive novice announcer could perform. My crossover jocks, "Paul Revere" on before me, and the guy I'll never be able to repay, "Tom Jefferson," who came in to start his show at seven, were a big part of my introduction to and education in radio.

I quickly learned that part of the fun of live radio for the experienced professional was trying to make the less experienced professional break up or make mistakes on the air. Perhaps you've heard stories about disk jockeys trying to make their news announcers crack while reading serious news. Like setting their news copy on fire or undressing them or themselves while the newscaster has no choice but to continue reading. Sure management frowns on such antics, but that doesn't stop us from trying.

I still have lunch occasionally with "Paul Revere," known, loved and named no doubt by his mother as Walt Fritz. And I remind him of the pranks he frequently pulled on the new kid, just to keep me on my toes. If there's anything I miss about the days of live radio (most of what you hear today is pre-recorded or "voice tracked"), it's the interaction between the jocks when shifts were changing. Some stations would even have the jocks talking to one another as they crossed. If you think your favorite personality is funny on his or her own, just imagine what happens when there are two of them in the studio at the same time! Over time, this led to the "morning crew" phenomenon, when your favorite morning show was a team of professionals, not a sole disk jockey.

Since I don't remember there being a second microphone in the main studio at WSNY, we didn't have this crossover talk between shifts. But when you have a joker like Walt handing over the wheel, you have to keep your eyes peeled and ears perked for fear of sounding stupid during your first music break after the top of the hour newscast. This was prime practical joker time for Walt.

One day, I vividly remember thinking he'd left the studio as I started my shift. He may have even opened the studio door to make it sound like he left. Or perhaps he left and snuck back in. But the way the studio was situated, I couldn't see that he was behind an equipment rack in the middle of the room. So when I opened the microphone to give a brief weather forecast, Walt appeared at the other end of the boom stand that was holding my mic and started pulling on the end of it. Through the laws of physics, this caused my mic to start inching away from me while I was talking on the air. But I didn't lose it. I just followed the mic and climbed up on the control board desk and then the board itself with forecast in hand and kept reading until I finished with the current temperature. I then dropped back down to the floor and hit the button for the next event and turned off my microphone. He was laughing harder than I was because I had actually kept my cool and didn't break on the air. He was impressed. I felt accepted.

But that didn't keep him from trying a different tactic some time later that summer. The reason you see radio announcers wearing headphones when they talk, is that the monitor speakers in the studio automatically mute when the microphone is turned on. That keeps the microphone from feeding back into the speakers and creating the squelching sound you occasionally hear in concert or live amplified events: feedback.

So it's important that in order for you to speak at the end of one event on the air, like a song that's fading out or ending, that you have your headphones on and the volume comfortably set. There's usually a volume control for your headphones near the jack where you plug them in. In the WSNY studios, a second jack had been installed *behind* the announcer for some reason. Perhaps with the thought there'd eventually be another microphone for a guest to use. However, the volume control for that headphone jack also controlled the volume of the main announcer's headphones. Good old Walt knew this before I did, and one day while I was speaking live on the air, he snuck into the studio behind me and started slowly turning up my headphone volume.

Once again, trying not to be thrown by this practical joker, I kept talking until I couldn't stand the volume in my ears any longer, and quickly pulled my headphones from my ears, immediately creating the aforementioned squealing feedback on the air. If I had simply unplugged the headphones, no one would have been the wiser, but I didn't think of that. Walt got another good laugh and I learned another good lesson. But I also wondered, "Why, if my boss always catches me making mistakes on the air, wasn't he listening when Walt was playing these jokes on me?" Probably because Walt knew when he could get away with it without the boss hearing us.

I alluded earlier to the vocabulary lessons I was getting from the more "adult" employees at the station. I use that term loosely because most Top 40 talent of the time were just kids in adult bodies. So the use of four letters words off the air to shock the new kid on the block was commonplace. I avoided copying this behavior for fear that I'd accidentally use a bad word on the air, which could end one's career quite quickly. But Walt loved the colorful abuse of the English language and salted four-letter words into his off-air patter all the time.

One day as I entered the studio toward the end of his shift, the music went silent as Walt turned his microphone on to begin a break and the speakers muted. He started out as we all did, saying "1240/WSNY and the latest from The Bee Gees…" and he continued on with, "That song really sucks and the f'ing brothers Gibb are really sh*%$y singers, so stand by from some f'ing great sh%* from the Beatles next!" Well, you could have knocked me over if you breathed on me at that point. I thought he'd truly lost his mind. Then he turned his mic off and I heard the Bee Gees still singing their song. Walt had not turned his mic to the on-air position, but instead to the "audition" channel on the control board. No one listening to the radio heard anything except the Bee Gees song he was playing. But the mic still mutes the in-studio monitor speakers, so he had once again shocked the jock who was only 17 and hoping to survive this hazing to remain on the radio until at least his 18th birthday.

Chapter
"**Eight** Days a Week" by The Beatles (1964)

You remember the summer of '69 (yes, it was in all the newspapers). Little did I realize as I started my career during the last summer of the 60s how eventful the summer would be for America and the world. It would end in the early fall with the hapless New York Mets winning their first World Series title, something deemed quite improbable when the season started. But before that surprise, two other events that summer helped make my first weeks on the radio quite unforgettable.

The first was on Sunday, July 20th, when two of the three men who had left planet Earth a few days before from Cape Kennedy, landed and eventually walked on our moon. I was watching TV at home when the landing actually happened, getting ready to head into the studios to work the six to midnight shift. My work schedule that summer was 3 to 7pm Monday through Saturday, plus Sunday evenings. I did not complain about working seven days a week, I would have worked eight days a week if the Beatles' idea had been taken seriously. That's how much I wanted to be in the studio every waking moment of my life as a rookie.

On the air at 4:17pm EDT that Sunday in July was my friend and mentor Tom Jefferson. He decided it would be great to play the song "Get Together" by the Youngbloods at the moment the Eagle landed, since the whole world was watching, despite all our differences. He noted the event on the label of the 45 single in the studio. When we played that record as an oldie, we often (proudly) mentioned it was the song we played when the world came together to watch the moon landing.

By the time I got to work at six o'clock, anticipation was high as to when the first steps to be taken by man on a foreign orb would happen. My friend and colleague "Chet Arthur," born Phil Blanchard, was in the newsroom that evening. I believe he was my age or perhaps even a tad younger and was just learning the business. For this historic evening, he brought in a portable black & white TV, because most newsrooms did not have such devices as standard equipment at the time. It wasn't lost on us that we would be reporting history throughout the evening, if indeed, Neil Armstrong could find his space suit and a ladder.

Phil was bringing news bulletins and updates into my studio during the evening, and I was reporting on preparations being made for the moon walk in between songs. Finally, at 10:56pm EDT, I broke into my music with the bulletin that Armstrong had stepped on the lunar surface and uttered the immortal words, "That's one giant step for (a) man, one giant leap for mankind." While Phil was able to witness it live on the TV in the newsroom, I remember not being able to see it because I was spinning records in the next room. I would see a replay when I arrived home after my Dad picked me up at midnight.

At least I had the presence of mind to bring home some souvenirs from the evening: Printed bits of newswire copy from the UPI teletype machine located in the hall just outside the newsroom. While Phil absconded with the most important bulletins and the F*L*A*S*H of Armstrong's quote, I got a few important pieces of wire copy that I've kept all these years. One particularly interesting piece of paper has my handwritten note from a phone call I got from our boss, Don DeRosa, moments after Armstrong strode on the lunar surface. He said, for the next hour, I want you to do every time check on the air followed by the words, "WSNY First Man on the Moon" time.

I know, it sounds corny in retrospect, but come on. This is 1969. America is at war in Vietnam, disgruntled students are marching in the streets in protest, terrorists are hijacking jet airliners out of the sky, bombs are going off in government buildings across our country and we're all wrestling with ring around the collar. For a few minutes in the middle of the summer of '69, the world is breathing, cheering and praying in unison, celebrating our generation's biggest achievement. We needed this.

The other historic event of this unique summer came just three weeks later, when more than 400,000 music lovers gathered peacefully in a farmer's field in Bethel, NY to listen to live music by some of the biggest acts in rock n' roll at the time. I'd like to tell you that the reason I wasn't at Woodstock is that I had to work on the radio that weekend, but the truth is even if I had asked for the weekend off, my parents would never have allowed me to go. And to be honest, for my position as a radio DJ, I was woefully uninformed about the event in the days leading up to the pilgrimage many made. I really don't remember thinking about it at all until it was all over the news that the event drew many times more people than anyone ever expected.

I do remember that my younger brother Scott, then almost 15, had been picked up from our house on Saturday morning of the "three days of peace, love and music" by our grandparents to spend the coming week at their home in Orange County, NY, just across the Hudson River from where the rock 'n roll music fans of the world were meeting. When he got home he reported that since the New York State Thruway was closed due to the unexpected traffic, they had taken an alternate, slower state highway where he witnessed many hippies walking along the road to Mecca, including one young man clad just in a huge diaper.

My first brush with unemployment came in the fall of 1969, some three months into my radio career. Once I started my senior year of high school, I could no longer continue working seven days a week. So I was relegated to Sunday's on the radio. I would start at 10am to babysit the control room while the hosts of the Polish and Italian hours played their music and spoke in languages I'd never heard in full sentences before. At noon I would take the station back to our Top 40 format and play good old rock n' roll until 6pm. The hours were long, but at least the pay was lousy. And I was still having fun! My friends from school would listen and some even called in requests that I'd play for them. This guaranteed a good seat in the cafeteria Monday in school. It was a win-win.

My only responsibility between 10am and 12 noon on Sundays at the station was to make sure we stayed on the air, that the meter readings got logged every half-hour and that I read the brief weather forecast and played the recorded legal identification around 11am, between these two time-honored community-service programs. I did this in my native language, English, which always made me wonder how many people listening in between the Polish and Italian hours actually understood what I was saying.

The key to keeping the flow between the programs was simple. I just needed the latest weather forecast and temperature, and to have the legal ID ready to play in the cart machine. The only flaw in this planning was the three-step process it took to play pre-recorded carted content on the air. Not only did you have to insert the cartridge into the machine, but you had to pull a lever forward that moved the rubber flywheel in the machine toward the capstan that would then engage when you pressed the start button. If you failed to do this, pushing the start button would accomplish nothing. If you pulled the lever and then hit the start button too quickly, the cart would "wow" in, just like records that weren't cued properly. In radio parlance, these were "mistakes."

If all of this sounds technical, it's really not. A kid can do it. And I was a kid. So I would perform this function many times throughout my hours on the air, without mishap. But for some reason this Sunday morning, I forgot to pull that lever to make the cart ready to play. So once I said, "...and it's 57 degrees at the Albany County Airport" to end my live portion of the break, I pushed the start button on the cart machine and the legal ID did not play. I hit it a second time, because that always works, right? And still nothing. So I muttered out loud, "What the hell?" And it went out live on the air! I know it did. I heard it in my headphones! I had uttered a swear word on the radio! My career was over.

I quickly turned my mic off, noticed my problem with the cart machine, pulled the lever and immediately punched the start button and heard "Dooouuuble-you-S-N-Y, Schenectady." Wow: the sound the cart made and my state of affairs at that moment. Wow, my radio career is over. At the ripe old age of 17.

Then, a funny thing happened. Nothing. In an era when a uttering a stray "hell" or "damn" was against FCC rules and regulations, and we had to edit out the word "Christ" from The Beatles' "Ballad of John and Yoko" in order to get the record on the air, I received not one phone call, not one complaint about my use of H-E double hockey sticks. Now there are probably some very reasonable reasons for this. First, I was uttering an English swear word in between two foreign language programs. Second, I did so on a Sunday morning when most religious folk were in church learning how *not* to go to hell. And third, the small audience listening really didn't care.

I mean, not even a call from my boss! Thank God. So after turning all shades of red and eating my 15-cent hamburger with 10-cent fries from the local Carroll's Hamburger fast-food joint, I was calm, cool and collected when I started my air shift at noon. Of course the lesson from all of this is two-fold: 1) Always be careful with your language when in a radio studio, whether you think the mic is on or not. And more importantly, 2) Remember your audience is always smaller and more apathetic than you think.

Chapter
"**Nine** in the Afternoon" by Panic! At the Disco (2008)

In my life I'm only aware of a couple of instances where I've influenced others with my work on the radio. One of these happened very early in my career, when my neighbor Dale Witkowski decided to build his own home radio station, influenced by what he saw me do in my basement to get ready for full-time work in my chosen industry. Dale is the oldest of two boys in his family, so his parents had a bit more disposable income to use on their son's new hobby. All of his equipment was better than mine, from the quieter toggle switches he used on his control board to the fact that he had TWO rather new cassette players wired into his set-up. That made it easier for him to play two songs back-to-back and even insert some recorded commercials in-between songs.

I'm proud to say Dale asked me to record some voice "drops" for his new station, WKTK (I assume representing the family name, Witkowski. So over the instrumental portion of "Beginnings," by Chicago Transit Authority, I recorded something like "Welcome to the new sound of radio in Scotia, WKTK. It's only the beginning!" My first non-paid radio imaging work, which I still do for friends today. In fact, today Dale (with a new last name, Linden), runs an Internet radio station on which you'll hear me twice an hour helping to position the music mix he plays on Soundirection FM 101, Washington, D.C. This is how Dale feeds his radio addiction, since he learned quite a lot faster than I, that few radio disk jockeys do not get rich solely by holding down a full-time radio announcer's job.

After a few short years trying to achieve that fete, Dale got smart, went back to college and got a degree that resulted in a long career in the FBI. Now retired, he makes more money as a part-time consultant than I ever made full-time on the radio.

Back in the past…my next few months of Sunday radio work went by rather uneventfully. I did make my first public appearance as Jesse James during the early fall of 1969. The station connected with our local teenage listeners through a garage band contest we called the "Boss Band" competition. Listeners were encouraged to vote each evening by phone for their favorite local band, and the top three vote-getting bands at the end of each month would be invited to play at the "WSNY Boss Band Dance" in a local community hall. All the available DJs from the station would host the event and meet with their legions of fans. By legions, I mean a dozen or so, of course.

Throughout my junior and senior high school years I acted in a number of drama club offerings, from comedies to musicals to dramas. So I wasn't afraid of being in front of an audience, and I remember my hosting chores going rather well. But I remember at one point in the evening while crossing the dance floor, which was quite vacant, my old friend Tom Jefferson was calling out my name to get my attention over the volume of the winning bands that were performing. He yelled out, at least a couple of times he tells me, "Jesse!" "Jesse!" Finally, in frustration, he called out "WARREN!" That finally got my attention. Evidently, I wasn't programmed quite yet to respond to my air name.

The remaining winter of 1969-70 was a senior year filled with announcing Saturday afternoon home games from the booth above the crowded bleachers of our high school football field, attending classes I didn't care much about, and acting in a supporting role in the stage production of "The Diary of Anne Frank." I also co-hosted and helped write skits for the school's annual talent show, "Spartan Spotlight," in the spring.

As my high school career was drawing to a close, I was accepted at the only college I had applied to, the now defunct Grahm Junior College, in Boston. Originally opened in 1950 as a secretarial school with 9 students called the Cambridge School of Business, during the mid-1960s the school started to build a rather reputable broadcasting curriculum. By 1970, more than 1,200 students, who like me, couldn't yet get into a four-year college, were enrolled as business or broadcasting majors. Among the broadcasting choices were radio and television performance and production and broadcast journalism. Graduates earned an Associates Degree. Since I already had experience in radio performance, I decided perhaps broadcast journalism as a major with a minor in TV production would round out my education in the business in which I wanted to spend my life. Who knew? I might become the next Walter Cronkite.

I remember thinking, with a little prodding from my boss and colleagues at WSNY, that since I was already in the business, I really didn't need to get a college education. I was already in the business of my choice! I believe everyone I worked with at the station had high school diplomas, nothing more. However, I had a feeling this argument wasn't going to fly with my folks. I was going to be the first person in our family's history to attend college, and it was a big deal. I specifically remember mentioning to my Uncle Charlie (the sage in our family, since he was the oldest) during my graduation party in June of 1970, that I wasn't sure why I was going off to college. He replied, in his usual short and to-the-point prose, "For your parents." Boston, here I come.

But first, there was the summer to enjoy! Since I was still working weekends at the station, I thought my weekdays would be spent lounging about, not having to worry about classes or homework for 10 weeks. But my mother had other ideas. She pointed out that if I wanted any money with which to go off to Boston, I should earn it myself. Imagine. The gall! So she arranged for me to work for a few weeks during the summer at the soft drink bottling plant where she worked in the office. Of course, I would work on the production line, making the usual minimum wage. But I could have as much soda as I could consume at lunch every day. Not a bad perk for a skinny college-bound kid very fond of root beer.

I remember thinking that this summer job was going to be quite a step down from my lofty career in radio. And while it was a bit more physical than jockeying disks, it wasn't bad. I tried to keep thinking about all the extra cash I'd have when I got to Boston, my first time in a big city. The deal was that I would work during July and the beginning of August, but that I'd be available to work at WSNY for the last two weeks of August, for the vacationing overnight announcer, John Paul Jones. (Go Young Americans!). Mr. Jones was born Don Bowers, just a year or so before I, with a voice that started in his big toe and echoed up his six-foot plus frame with a reverberation that left no doubt he was born to be a radio announcer. If you told me when I was 18 that I'd have the pleasure of working with Don again some 40 years later, at the end of my working life, I would have had you committed. He, like I, left full-time radio to work in sales and marketing, and our paths converged in 2007 when I became the first marketing director at a voice acting training company. We worked together for almost 11 years, before I retired from full-time work. Funny how life works. He turned out to be the bookends of my working life.

Working the midnight shift on radio is quite a unique experience. This was the only time in my career that I'd work such a shift live on the air. But sounding alive on the air in the middle of normal-people sleeping hours means having to find considerable time to sleep during the daylight hours, something young, vacationing brothers and sisters were not necessarily interested in assisting you with.

At least by now I had my driver's license and the loan of my mother's car in which to make my way in and out of Schenectady for a couple of weeks. I actually learned how to record my show off the air for posterity, and stealing a couple of certainly unwanted 7" reels of recording tape from the production studio, I still have airchecks of a couple of hours of my substitute work during Don's vacation. And I also had the presence of mind to record the final hour of my last live show on 1240/WSNY. I believe it was the Sunday of Labor Day weekend, and for the first time I prepared some thoughts about my first 14 months in radio to share with my last Sunday afternoon audience prior to college.

I chose a few oldies that highlighted my time on the station, planned to refer to a couple of girlfriends I'd had during my tenure, and prepared for a sunny farewell at 6:00pm. Only one problem. My body and mind were still on the midnight shift schedule. I was doing my last show during the hours I had been sleeping for the previous two weeks. So, to put it plainly, I was not completely present for my final shift on the station. Something that didn't go unnoticed by the station's general manager, who happened to be in his office down the hall from my studio, working, for some reason, on a Sunday afternoon.

At least a couple of times during my first hour on the air that afternoon, I gave a time check saying it was after 12 AM instead of PM. This didn't sit well with the 49% owner of our station, who never attended the Don DeRosa School of Broadcasting. He didn't know about the rule that you should never correct or yell at an announcer during his hours on the air. So, after my second (or maybe third) mistaken time check, he burst into my studio and yelled at me, "Why can't you get the f*&%ing time right!?" I responded the way any normal, 18-year-old screw-up would in the face of a much older, more important, and more importantly, correct boss would. I apologized profusely, and assured him it wouldn't happen again.

Had I had a bit more time to think about a better response, it would have gone quite a bit differently. This guy had never been on the radio. He was a businessman, and I believed he really had no idea what it took to do what I was doing. He also had regular sleeping hours, I'm sure, and didn't realize what my schedule had been for the last two weeks. If I hadn't spent time preparing for my last afternoon on the radio, and if I hadn't known that a lot of my family and friends were listening this special day, I know I would have looked him in the eye, unplugged my headphones and handed them to him saying, "Here. You do it!" How could he have responded? He couldn't fire me, it was my last day. And he couldn't do it himself, because he wasn't a real broadcaster.

But cooler heads prevailed. After my dressing down, I was now really quite awake, and the rest of the afternoon went smoothly, if you don't count the mistake I made when I went into the production studio to start the tape deck that would record the final hour of my show. When I started the recorder, I missed a step that would actually insure I'd be recorded. I won't get into the technicalities, but suffice it to say, when I went back into the studio at 5:30 (thank God) to check on my aircheck, I notice the mistake, swore loudly, corrected my error, and was able to capture my final half hour on the air. Nothing like going out with a bang!

Chapter
"Ten Little Indians" by Nilsson (1967)

When I began this writing exercise, I thought the story of my first radio job would consume many more words and pages than they have to this point. Life sure seemed longer. But noticing the length so far, I believe I may just continue sharing stories of my days of college radio and the ensuing years of full-time radio employment. Don't worry, only 16 more years to go. There certainly are some more interesting characters to introduce you to, and it's still too wet and cold to go outside, even though it's the end of April as I compose this. Winter just won't let go. It snowed again today in the mountains in the region. And since there's no place to add anti-freeze in my lawn mower, I can't yet try to start it up for the season. So, if you're game, I'll take us to the next chapter. My college year. (Yeah, "year." I'll explain later).

Some of the highlights to look forward to: Seeing my dad cry for the first time, meeting a future number one recording artist before anyone knew his name, and what fast food hot dog stands to avoid in Boston's Kenmore Square in 1970. How you'll apply that last nugget of knowledge is beyond me, but let's continue our time travel.

I originally looked into attending Grahm Junior College at the suggestion of my high school guidance counselor. He said it would be perfect for a guy like me. A guy with questionable grades and unquestionable verbal talent. He obviously hadn't listened to me on the radio. But he knew about my love for it, and knew that the academic standards at Grahm wouldn't be a large hurdle for me to clear. I wouldn't have to take a language or math or science. Hey, what's not to love? Of course, if he had explained to me that Western Civilization, Psychology and Sociology classes could be my undoing, I might have reconsidered continuing education entirely.

But I was really looking forward to my Broadcast Journalism, Introduction to Radio Performance, and TV Production classes, taught by actual former radio and television professionals-turned-educators. And I'd be lying if I said getting out of our house, away from brothers and sisters whom I was still being asked to babysit for more often than I cared to, wasn't also among my reasons for heading to Boston. And then there was that little conflict called Vietnam that I could avoid by being a student. For the time-being, anyway.

So it was off to "Beantown," home of this Yankees' fan's be-hated Boston Red Sox, who played just across I-90 from Kenmore Square, where the campus was centered. And where, if you could sneak up to the roof of our dorm (formerly the St. George's Hotel), you could see everything but the third base line inside Fenway Park. Cool.

I had done a tour of the college with my parents a few months before and actually met Milton Grahm, the college's president and namesake. About all I remember of that tour were the WCSB Radio studios, the college's closed-circuit radio station. Where, if you passed the audition, you could entertain the few hundred students back in their dorm rooms who remembered the college had a radio station. They couldn't get our signal on their transistor radios out in Kenmore Square, however, since "closed-circuit" means you had to have your radio plugged into the college's electrical system in order to pick up "Radio 640." But none of this bothered me. This was going to be my home away from dorm, and the equipment looked very similar to what I'd been using for my first few months in the business. Audition? Piece of cake.

But let's not get ahead of ourselves. In early September, mom and dad drove me to Boston, about a three-hour drive east from our home, to move me into my dorm room, meet my roommates, and have one last meal together before their first born became the family's first official college student. The afternoon was uneventful. I was assigned to a suite, two rooms, four beds, one bath. Two of my roommates were from Connecticut, and the other was from Maine. I only remember the name of one of those new (read: forced) friends, and that's only because he grew up to become a successful TV series producer. More on that later.

When it came time for mom and dad to leave for home, I was expecting mom to cry, but I wasn't expecting much, if any, emotion from dad. He was a hard-working automobile salesman who found a way to feed and clothe a family of six kids. He did this by working more than 60 hours a week, which meant we didn't see much of him. And when we did, he wasn't always in a great mood. He valued his down time and expected it to be quiet and non-confrontational. Too bad kids aren't built like that. He was known to raise his voice on occasion, but basically, he raised us the way he had been raised, with a firm hand which we firmly felt on occasion. Not one for praise, you considered yourself on track if he didn't yell at you. Not that we didn't love him. And we came to understand what it took to provide for such a family only after we'd all grown and started our own families. Isn't that often the way it works?

So when I noticed tears in my father's eyes (there's a country song title for you, no charge) as he said goodbye to me, it struck me and stuck with me. This was as big a deal for him as it was for me, maybe bigger. Uncle Charlie was right on target. This was dad's involuntary way of showing me love and pride, as he found it hard to express verbally. Thank God I'm more verbal, or I would be pursuing the wrong career.

So mom and dad left and I remember immediately feeling quite lonely, even with three new roommates to spend time with. All three were television majors, and I was radio. Not sure how that wasn't noticed in the hierarchy of the college's room assignment department, but there you go. Not that they weren't fun to get to know. But once we got to know each other, we knew it wasn't a great fit. I spent some time trying to meet others at a few college events and in the rathskeller, but nothing clicked until I auditioned for the college radio station.

However, it's notable that one of those roomies went on to a career in TV that has probably touched your life. Paul Fusco is quite a natural wit, and kept us all laughing even when we may have been a bit homesick at the start of our college careers. I remember once, after using the one vacuum cleaner available for our 4th floor dorm room, he threw it back onto our RA's room yelling, "This thing SUCKS!" Well, I thought it was funny. It stuck with me all these years.

But Paul was destined for even funnier moments in his life about a decade later as the creator, writer and voice of everyone's favorite alien life form from Melmac, ALF, on NBC-TV. The story is that he walked into network president Brandon Tartikoff's office for the sitcom pitch with the ALF puppet on his arm and promptly disarmed the amused decision-maker.

When the show debuted in 1986, our two sons were 7 and 5, so were were squarely in front of the set when ALF landed and tried to eat his host family's cat, quite a delicacy on Melmac, I'm told. My boys loved the premise and the show. While watching the credits in weeks to come, I noticed "Paul Fusco" on the screen and mentioned to my wife that I had a roommate in college with that name. A few weeks later I found out it indeed was the Paul who made me laugh so much years before. When I mailed him a congratulations note, he replied with a couple of "autographed" color photos of ALF, featuring a paw print under the boys' names.

Needless to say, I found my element when I finally met other radio majors. We all had one immediate goal: a good, regular shift on WCSB, Radio 640. Our program director was one Doug Neatrour (don't try to pronounce it, just call him by his professional air name, Jay Douglas). Doug is from Pennsylvania and was a big fan of Philadelphia radio, which influenced his on-air and program directing styles. We got along immediately as he took me into a studio down the hall from the radio station to audition for a regular air shift.

Now if you remember all the way back to when I failed at my first attempt to obtain a third class broadcasting license, you'll remember my fear of tests. Hate 'em. Never do well, even to this day. If there was a written test about food before I was allowed to eat breakfast, I'd be 40 pounds thinner. I'm not sure how I passed my written driver's license test at 18. So my 15 months of radio experience was all for naught, because I performed quite terribly when I was asked to ad-lib a few record intros in front of my new boss. If only he had asked to hear one of my radio airchecks of what I sounded like on WSNY, I think I would have been his top choice for afternoon drive-time jock. Been there, done that. But instead, I earned myself a two-hour weekly Saturday morning shift, on the air from 9 to 11am.

Of course, this meant I had to actually attend all the classes expected of a freshman seeking an associates degree between

Monday and Friday, and be satisfied with a couple of weekend hours when everyone in the dorm was still sleeping off Friday night's party. My solution to this dilemma, was to remind Doug I was actually a broadcast journalism major, and could handle some newsroom shifts during the week, especially after my last class of the day. That's how I became the co-anchor of "Evening Newsbeat," a half-hour of news, sports, weather, and public affairs information each weekday evening at six. My co-anchor was one Steve Martin. No, not THAT Steve Martin. Not that he wasn't a nice Steve Martin. We got along fine. He had (and still does, last we talked) a great, powerful voice, which later served him well through a long, successful career in broadcast journalism in Washington, DC.

Then unknown Steve and I would hit the newsroom no later than 5pm nightly to construct a half-hour combination of newswire stories and original pieces we re-wrote from the Boston newspapers. It was a terrific training ground, where we put into practice what we learned during the day in "Introduction to Broadcast Journalism" class, a couple floors up from the basement radio station.

By the way, this is where the air name "Chris Warren" was first introduced to the unsuspecting radio listening world. (Thank you, Robin). Actually, I believe I used "Christopher Warren" on the newscasts during the week, and shortened it to Chris for my jock shift on Saturdays. Not sure what I thought this would accomplish, except to confuse both me and the listener as to who I really was. This arrangement repeats itself later in my career. Stay tuned.

I'm happy to say that after a week or two of my Saturday jock shift, my boss Doug came into the studio and said, "You're quite good. Why didn't you sound that way on your audition?" This gave me hope for the second semester, when there would again be auditions for the station and a reconfiguring of the jock shifts. After

Christmas break, Doug, who was now my roommate, told me I was done co-anchoring Evening Newsbeat and was now going to follow it, with a shift from 6:30 to 10:00pm nightly. This was the longest and one of the more prestigious shifts on our closed-circuit station, that we promoted as "Total Radio." By this time of the evening students were back in their dorm rooms and available as an audience. Of course, we had no way of measuring our reach and once, when we tried to do a call-in contest, we got little response. The station was truly a training ground for future radio personalities. The only thing we didn't learn was how to answer listeners calls while we were on the air. There weren't any.

While most of us played Top 40 music, we also had jocks with jazz, heavy metal (also known as "underground" music), folk and easy listening formats. Thus, "Total Radio." Pretty clever for a bunch of post-pubescent boys who liked to play disk jockey. But my format was the one I loved and was the most familiar with: The Top 40 hits of the day plus about four "oldies" an hour. I also became the production director of the station, responsible for the recorded portions of our programming like commercials, promotional announcements and the jingles you hear leading into the music. Yes, believe it or not, we had a sales department that tried selling air time on a closed-circuit radio station. And while we only had a couple of regular accounts, it was great training. Our college bookstore and a diner/deli adjacent to our communications building in Kenmore Square were the regular customers I recall. Not sure what they paid, but "a dollar a holler" comes to mind.

Chapter
"**Eleven** O'Clock Tick Tock" by U2 (1983)

While I was enjoying many more hours at the radio station when I should have been either going to sociology or psychology classes or at least doing homework assignments, I had a bit of a social life. For a time I kept in touch with my girlfriend from high school, but long-distance relationships are hard to maintain, especially when one can't afford to make long distance telephone calls as a poor college student. So as not to bore you completely, I've shied away from including my love life in much of this narrative. Until I met my wife of more than 40 years during my final years in full-time radio, there's not much that's funny or interesting about those relationships. Hey, if this radio-themed book is a big seller, then maybe my next one will be a personal tell-all. Hope you're not holding your breath.

Some of the highlights of my evenings on WCSB: Having the Friday evening 10 o'clock newscast written and read by a very drunk newsman (we started drinking early in those days)…getting upset at the college hockey team whose matches we aired live from Boston Garden, when their game would dig into the first hour of my shift…and introducing new music to our "audience," when the music director would come bursting into the studio and say, "Here! You have to play this new Carpenter's single! It's going to be a smash!" Our music director, Ted Hayward, from New Brunswick, Canada, was very proud of the fact that he had built good relationships with the local record company representatives, despite the fact that we had no audience we could measure as a closed-circuit college station.

Ted was in such good stead with the Boston record reps, that one day he brought an up-and-coming singer/songwriter into our communications building to record an interview with him. This artist was popular back in my neck of the woods, the upper Hudson River Valley of New York, having played at the famous folk club Café Lena in Saratoga Springs (which opened in 1960 and is still in business). This folk music haven helped introduce folks like Bob Dylan and Emmylou Harris to the world, and now Ted wanted me to meet it's newest find, who was about to release an album on a national record label.

So Ted pops into my studio one evening to introduce us, since this new artist is familiar with my hometown region. This young troubadour was very unassuming, kinda quiet and shy, so I didn't really think much more about him once he was led down the hall to a production studio for the interview taping. But about one year later, while working at my first radio station after college, I played a new single by this same gentleman called "American Pie." I remember being surprised that a song of this length was getting played on contemporary radio at all, but Don McLean certainly put his stamp on popular American music with his song about "the day the music died." And I met him when…

While I was live on the air in the basement student-run radio station, the TV performance and production majors were up on the third floor of our communications building, airing (closed-circuit, of course) a half-hour nightly newscast, and various live and recorded student projects and shows. In the early spring of 1971 some of my classmates would stop by while I was on the air to say hi, and quite a few said they were in the building to check out one of the students hosting a children's program on WCSB-TV. Evidently he invited local kids into the studio to be his live audience and played old cartoons and comedy shorts and did some stand-up comedy shtick that everyone was talking about.

They'd tell me, "You've got to check this guy out. He's weird but really funny!" And I always had the same response: "I'm busy playing two-and-a-half-minute songs on my show, how can I do that?" Finally, after hearing about this guy "Andy" for a few weeks, I put the Beatles' "Hey Jude" on the turntable, prayed it wouldn't skip or stick while it played for 7 minutes and 11 seconds, and dashed out the station door, up four flights of stairs (remember, we were in the basement), and burst into the control room for the student-run color-TV station. And there was the future Saturday Night Live guest and the character you loved as Latka on TV's "Taxi," Andy Kaufman, lip-syncing to the Mighty Mouse theme song playing on the record player next to him. The kids in the audience ate it up, as did Andy's fellow students watching from their dorm rooms. Just five years later, Andy would take to national television with his strange sense of humor.

A few months later I met a quite affable young man by the name of Marc Berkowitz, an incoming freshman who was majoring in TV performance and production. He joined a bunch of friends and I for a late night/early morning bite to eat at a local eatery called "Le Crepe." I believe it was on Boylston Street, a short walk from Kenmore Square. Marc entertained us with a great sense of humor and some simple magic tricks. When the check came he asked the waitress if we had to pay the bill if he could make it disappear before her eyes. She said, unfortunately, "Yes, I have a carbon copy." But Marc went ahead and impressed us all anyway, making it seemingly disappear from his hand. When we got up to leave, after squaring with the waitress, I spotted it crumpled up underneath our table. You may know this good-looking, talented man as the original host of

Nickelodeon's "Double Dare," and producer of many food-related television programs, Marc Summers.

Many other Grahm graduates went on to change the face of radio and TV in the 70s and 80s, some after getting four-year degrees at higher learning institutions. One was a co-founder of ESPN, a couple of others reached the pinnacle of Top 40 radio of the day when they worked at WABC in New York City, and still others started satellite radio networks and worked at some well-known and well-respected radio and TV stations around the country. Me? I left after my freshman year to pursue a full-time career in radio. This happened for a couple of reasons. First, a lot of what I'd been "learning" in my radio and broadcast journalism classes I had learned while on the job before I went away to college. I had more experience than most of my classmates, and I try not to be the kind to show off. So I was quite quiet in class, letting my fellow students "Learn by Doing," the motto of Grahm Junior College.

My other reason for leaving after just two semesters of higher education had to do with my moving out of the dorm. In the spring of 1971 I was given permission by the college to move off campus and rent an apartment nearby with two classmates, Steve Garsh and Marty Sheldon. This was usually against college policy, because they really needed room and board dormitory fees to help keep the institute afloat. But I was told it would be OK.

I was supposed to spend the summer as a paid college intern working in the press room at the office of the Mayor of Boston. Not too shabby. Unfortunately, somewhere in Washington, DC, they cut the budget that supported this program, and I was suddenly without a job for the summer, but still expected to pay my third of the rent. I quickly found a job ushering at a local first-run movie theater a couple of stops up the Green Line of the "T" from Kenmore Square.

Luckily, this only lasted two or three weeks, because the same movie played throughout my employment there. If you ever need to know the complete scripted dialog of "Love Story," just ask me. I still remember every scene. And remember, "Love means never having to say you're sorry."

Turns out the now-graduated former morning man on our college radio station was the foreman of the summer dorm-painting crew, and a few weeks into the summer he had a kid quit. He asked if I'd like to join the crew and I jumped at the chance. I would sorely miss the free popcorn from my ushering job, but would actually earn a bit more painting. And I learned a trade at the same time. If you ever need painting done around your house, I'm not bad. Just clear it with my wife first. She handles my painting schedule.

At summer's end when I went to sign up for fall semester classes, I was told I would have to move back into a dorm in order to attend. I explained that just this past spring I had been told I could live off campus and that I had signed a year's lease for the apartment and couldn't leave my friends without my share of the rent, but the school wouldn't budge from their rule. Even a plea from my parents didn't dissuade them. In time, I learned that the college was in a very poor financial condition that would lead to its demise just seven years later. I'm sure my dorm fee could have saved the school. I feel awful.

I really wanted to stay in Boston, where I had made new friends and had a fiduciary responsibility to two of them. So I started looking for full-time work on Boston radio. You would think that after working for 15 months at a real honest-to-goodness radio station, and honing my craft for another 9 months on college radio, that doors would be opening for me all across this great nation, or at least in Boston, the 6th largest radio market in the country. But alas, I spent the fall of 1971 working in the Sears catalog warehouse in Boston, just to make the rent. If you lived in the northeastern United States that fall and ordered any toys from the Sears Christmas Wish catalog, there's a chance I physically handled your order, as we shipped toys to all the good little boys and girls.

But this was also a scary time in my life, as I no longer had a student deferment from the draft. I was fair game for Uncle Sam's Selective Service cronies who couldn't get enough fresh bodies to send to Southeast Asia. This was always in the back of my mind as I roamed the warehouse stacks and made new friends in the world of work. I was making enough money to pay the rent, help with food and go out and party on occasion. I remember one co-worker was the first foreigner I ever met, one Ronan Twohig of Dublin, Ireland. While we only worked together for four or five months, I kept in touch with him for a year or two, before life got on the way and we lost contact. But I've never forgotten the name, which I guess is a popular one in Ireland, as I've found a few folks carrying it through life. Just not the one I drank with.

At the end of the holiday catalog rush I was moved into the men's socks department of the Sears warehouse, or at least that's all I remember packing and shipping in January. I knew this wasn't the life for me, but it wasn't easy looking and interviewing for radio work with a full-time job. So, to keep from going completely bonkers, I quit to spend my time concentrating on landing anything on the radio. I wasn't sure how long I'd be able to pay my third of the rent having no steady income, but I was confident that with more time to audition for a radio job, I would be employed soon.

Chapter
"**12**:30" by the Mamas and the Papas (1968)

I auditioned for a couple of Boston stations that winter while my dad searched for a cheap car for me that would allow me to look for work outside metro Boston. I remember auditioning by preparing and reading a newscast for a station that had studios at street level in busy downtown Boston. The news director asked if I'd rather he pull the shades down on the windows so I wouldn't be auditioning in front of curious passers-by, and I said yes, please. Didn't help. I didn't get the gig.

I also auditioned at a station with studios on Boston harbor called WJIB-FM. Jib, a sailing term, get it? Once again, my fear of tests (read: auditioning) reared its ugly head. What I remember most about the audition is the interviewer asking if I wanted to hear the recording of the newscast I had just read. When he played it back, I heard a clicking noise as I spoke, and had to ask the interviewer what that weird sound was on the recording. He said it was the noise my dry mouth was making as I read out loud into a very expensive microphone. This is how a 19-year-old radio star wannabe learns to bring water with him when he's going to be on mic. They never taught me this in college. All that money spent for nothing. And I didn't get the gig.

When dad delivered to me a black with red interior 1967 Ford Fairlane 500 (with red shag carpeting on the rear window shelf) in early January, I felt for sure I was now on the road to radio, so to speak. I don't remember how I paid for the gas, but I hit a few stations outside Boston and even drove to Hartford, CT to interview for a newscasting job at either WTIC or WDRC, I don't remember which. I didn't get the gig, which is probably why I don't remember which station it was.

During this time my father was convinced that part of the reason I wasn't getting hired at these stations wasn't that I wasn't good enough for the job, but that I had hair down over my ears. Of course, I looked like every other young person in America at the time, but he stressed that these weren't the folks that would hire me, they were men like him, who considered long hair disrespectful and unacceptable in the workplace. Of course I knew better and pooh-poohed his observation. But I wasn't getting work, and money was running out.

So I made the decision many post-college students made even back in the 1970s—I decided I had to move back home. I told my roomies that I would honor my lease and send them my $70 each month through the end of our contract in April, provided I could find work when I got home or could beg the money off my folks. All my earthly possessions in the year of my 20th birthday easily fit into the trunk and back seat of my car with room to spare. I left my new favorite city and my girlfriend of almost 10 months (later to be my first wife) in the rear view mirror as I headed west on I-90 back to the Capital District of New York.

I don't remember feeling odd about returning home. It seemed quite natural to me. My plan was to continue to look for radio work, but now I had mom and dad's income as back-up. Luckily, I didn't need it. At dad's continued urging, I gave in and visited my old friend Red the barber and got what I considered to be a healthy trim on my long locks, which hadn't been seriously cut since the summer of 1970. It wasn't shoulder length, but close. Dad insisted that upstate New York was very different from Boston, and long hair would keep me unemployable. After Red's professional handiwork, the bottom of my ears were now discernible, and while it didn't completely appease my father, I felt it was a good compromise.

I don't remember if I checked in with my old boss at WSNY to see if there was a position open there, but within a couple of days I had arranged interviews at two other Albany area radio stations, WHRL-FM in Troy and WKAJ AM/FM in Saratoga Springs. After months of rejections in Massachusetts and Connecticut, I immediately got offered jobs from both general managers at these two, small local stations. I could start the next week for $2.10 an hour in Troy, about a 40 minute drive from our house, or get $2.25 an hour in Saratoga, about a 30-minute drive. At least I was smart enough to accept the shorter drive/more pay offer from the Saratoga station. Only one proviso to landing my position there: Owner and general manager Kent Jones (the station was named after his young daughter Kimberly Ann Jones) said I'd have to get my hair cut. He said the small community of Saratoga Springs, famous around the world for summer thoroughbred racing and healing mineral spas, wasn't ready for a radio announcer with "hippie-like hair."

Yes, that's right. Go ahead and laugh. I certainly didn't when I told my father that I needed more money to get another haircut, two days after Red's generous trim. I'm not sure what I was more embarrassed about: admitting to my father that he was right, or having to go back to Red to have my hair cut even shorter. Since Red had been cutting my hair since I was about 12 years old, he took pity on this soon-to-be employable still-too-hairy boy, and didn't charge me. I don't think I had the sense or experience to at least offer him a tip. Sorry about that, Red.

So now, with about half of my ears showing, I was ready to get back to the business of broadcasting, albeit in a smaller, slightly outside-the-market AM/FM combo at 900 on the AM dial, and 101.3

FM. The AM station had to sign off at sunset to avoid interference with other stations in the region using nearby frequencies, but with the FM on until midnight, there were plenty of hours to go around the staff of five full-timers and a couple of part-timers. I was full-time, but worked Wednesday through Sunday, with the attractive days of Monday and Tuesday (when everyone else was working) to myself.

When I was hired, I told my new boss I used the professional air name of Chris Warren, which I felt was easier to understand than my given name. And since my dad's name was also Warren, it avoided confusion by local listeners, some of whom may have bought cars from my father. But Mr. Jones insisted that I use my real name on the air, since he didn't want his announcers to appear too "high falutin'" by taking on fake names. "We're a small market, personal station to our listeners," he explained. So on my third radio station, I used a third name: the one my parents gave me.

If my memory serves me correctly, which is no guarantee as I type this on our new covered patio on the rear of our home with no mortgage in beautiful suburban Guilderland, NY some 46 years later, my first shift started at 6:00 PM on a Sunday evening in February of 1972. I arrived at least an hour or two early to learn about what was expected of me from the part-timer working the Sunday afternoon shift, and at six I was ready to rumble. Which is exactly what I did.

During my first on-air break shortly after six, I opened the mic and identified the station and myself, and as I hit the button to start the record I had cued up on turntable two, I accidentally started up the spare turntable, number three. Now, since this was the spare turntable and wasn't used often, it was the perfect spot to place the large, glass ashtray used by the smoking DJs on the staff, which was everyone but me. So when the turntable started at 45 rpm, it whipped the ashtray across the floor, making a nice crashing sound. That was followed by me laughing and saying something stupid and then pushing the correct button to start turntable two.

Once I turned the mic off, the departing part-time DJ said, "We don't laugh and make fun of ourselves on this station. This is serious business." Now the reason I don't remember the name of this part-timer (I'm doubtful anyone does) is because that's the silliest statement I've ever heard about music radio. People tune in to radio for the psychological lift it gives them from the music and the air personalities they enjoy. It's Radio 101, one of the first things you have to understand in order to connect with the audience and keep them coming back. Jeesh.

After that somewhat auspicious start I settled in quickly playing what I guess would have been described as Middle-of-the-Road music, M-O-R. While we played some of the softer top pop hits of the day by folks like The Carpenters, the Fifth Dimension, Donny Osmond and the like, we mixed in classics from Frank Sinatra, Tony Bennett, Dean Martin, Ella Fitzgerald, etc. My music world was expanding! In fact, it expanded all the way to classical music. On Sunday evenings at 9:00 PM, the local bank sponsored an hour of classical music. I was told it would be easy. Just play a couple of sides of one of the classical albums in the quite meager classical collection, announcing at the beginning of the hour what selection it was, who composed it, and who was performing it.

Only one small problem. I didn't know the first thing about classical music. And vinyl albums of the day contained about 20 to 25 minutes of music per side. So at about 9:45 or 9:50 every Sunday evening you'd hear me faking a second introduction to a short movement that would fill in the final few minutes of the sponsored hour. Now, growing up in our house there wasn't evidence of any classical music. In fact, until I started buying rock n' roll records in the mid-60s, there weren't any records of any kind in our home. We didn't have a family record player, just my 45 RPM affair in the basement hooked up to my quarter-watt radio station. The extent of my classical music education was tuning past Leonard Bernstein's "Young Peoples Concerts" on TV. I was lucky I knew how to pronounce Beethoven, because when you look at it it's Beat Hoven, right? Imagine my fun trying to pronounce Prokofiev. I think it came out Proko-Five. Thank God no one was listening. Or if they were, that they didn't have the radio station's phone number to call in a complaint.

Chapter
"13 Beaches" by Lana Del Rey (2017)

While working at WKAJ I got the chance to do a little bit of everything. If you were the morning DJ, you did the news when your shift was done, so you could get a full eight hours of work into your day. Conversely, if you were the mid-day DJ you were expected to do the morning news. I was fortunate enough to work each of those shifts in my 15 months in Saratoga, in addition to writing, voicing and producing the occasional commercial or station promotional announcement (promo). This is what radio was in the smaller market days of the early 1970s, and I was loving it.

I got the chance to spend some of my Saturdays in the fall broadcasting the Saratoga Springs High School football games on the air, as well. While I had done some booth announcing as sporting events at my high school, this was a very different animal. This consisted of keeping the airwaves full of interesting information between the plays. Luckily, I wasn't responsible for the play-by-play, but I was the "color man," the second guy in the announcer booth, who explains who just did what on the field, and what might be coming up next, in my less-than-expert opinion.

I don't remember doing any of the preparation that today's announcers certainly do before a broadcast. I remember being handed the day's program, just like everyone else at the game, and hoping the players' uniforms stayed clean enough to be able to read their jersey numbers. And then you had to hope that not only was the printed roster correct, but that the players were wearing their assigned jerseys! I'm sure there were listeners at home that knew when I messed up, because their football son was home sick or with a broken leg that day, but again, the phone never rang.

Mostly I remember the fall of 1972 being quite cold, so that instead of sitting on top of the station remote vehicle, or the "pie wagon," as we called it, because it really was an old bakery deliver truck repainted with a heavy wooden deck now adorning the top, we were inside the truck to avoid freezing to death. You know how hard it is to concentrate and keep your mouth moving when your teeth want to chatter you're so cold? Inside the truck we had a space heater, which on really cold days would steam up the window we were looking through in order to call the game! Where else but in small town radio can you have these kinds of memories? And challenges?

At the ripe old age of 20 (40 in disk jockey years), I wasn't allowed to actually drive the pie wagon to remotes and ballgames. The excuse I was given was that with the top-heavy platform on top of the truck, management was worried I'd take a corner a bit too fast and tip the thing over. But as I proved myself capable both on the air and off, I was soon piloting the vehicle to events and remote broadcasts in the greater Saratoga region. I remember one remote in particular in that chilly fall that was designed to bring our listeners to the grand opening of a new hardware store just outside the city. The store wasn't large enough for us to set up any equipment inside, so I parked the vehicle in the parking lot in front of the store and turned the flashing yellow lights on top of the truck on to attract as much attention as possible. Inside the unit I was spinning records and talking about the new business to our radio audience, when the owner of the store suddenly opened the door to my studio-on-wheels and handed me a nice cold beer (I remember it was my first Heineken), "…to warm you up," he said.

Now I'm pretty sure there's something in the FCC rules and regulations outlawing "drinking and broadcasting," but darned if I remembered where it was written down I couldn't imbibe. And it was going to be a couple more hours before I'd climb behind the wheel to bring the unit back to the station, so I happily sipped it to completion. Oh yeah, didn't I say I was 20 years old at the time? New York had recently raised the drinking age from 18 to 21, so in any event, it was still illegal. Not to mention the trouble I'd be in if the station owner came by to see how the broadcast was going. A few years later at another of my stops on my radio road, I caught the general manager of the station downing a six-pack of brew while doing a summer Saturday evening air shift, so I eventually felt vindicated.

As I alluded to a while back, when you work at a small town, low-wattage radio station you wear a lot of hats. After a few months of Wednesday to Sunday shifts, I was promoted to Monday through Saturday mid-day host. But this meant I would be researching, writing and reading five minute news reports every half-hour from 6:30 to 9:00am. Now, by "researching," I mean re-writing the news reported in the local newspaper, The Saratogian. This is a time-honored tradition, where low-paid newspaper reporters did all the work, and all the local low-paid radio news people had to do was re-write the story so it wasn't immediately apparent what the source of the story was. If you were good enough, the newspaper didn't catch on. Since I was rather inexperienced and not very good at creative journalism, I was called on the carpet a couple of times by the station owner, who was good friends with the publisher of the Saratogian.

The boss decided that I should do some of my own original reporting, which meant I would get up even earlier in the morning than I already regretted, allowing time for me to stop by the Saratoga

Springs Police Department on my way to work and read the police reports of the previous 12 hours, since our last newscast of the day at 6 the previous evening. This proved to be a great way to keep our finger on the pulse of Saratoga, despite the fact that unless it was August, when the Saratoga Thoroughbred Track season brought thousands of seasonal residents to town, there wasn't much activity that the police had to deal with.

I do remember two specific incidents from those police reports. One was when I learned that a member of my high school senior class was killed in a motorcycle accident just south of the city overnight. Trying to separate your professional and personal feelings reporting a story like that is not easy, but I plowed through.

Another incident involved a motor vehicle death that wasn't. I swear to this day that when I read the accident report at police headquarters, it indicated that the driver of the vehicle had died in the accident. This was quickly dispelled when at about 6:35 that morning, after I had read the name of the supposedly deceased driver on the air, the overnight desk sergeant called the station to ask where I got my information. When I told him it was on the police report I read about an hour earlier at his desk, he said "Absolutely not. No fatalities overnight." Being raised to respect my elders, especially police elders, I corrected my story for the next newscast and apologized on the air for my mistake. Once again I'm on the worn-out carpeting in my boss's office shortly after 8 that morning, explaining myself. He rightfully suggested that in the future it might not be a bad idea to confirm any suspected deaths gleaned from police reports with the desk sergeant while I was in his presence. You learn something new every day.

So, you're asking yourself when I got a chance to eat, if I was working from 6 to 9am in the newsroom, followed by a four hour disk jockey shift. No need to ask yourself, because only I have the answer. The magic hour of 9am is when I slipped out of the station for about 30 minutes to grab a bite. My favorite stop was McDonald's, where they had just introduced the best breakfast sandwich known to man, or at least radio people, the Egg McMuffin. The only problem was that back then, McDonald's stopped serving breakfast at 9am. So when I arrived about ten minutes after the hour, I had to pray they still had one or two under the heat lamp. When they didn't, it was the old 25-cent hamburger and 15-cent fries (inflation since my early days in the business, 4 years before).

The summer of '72 I met one of those "most unforgettable characters" you used to read about in the old Reader's Digest magazine. You remember magazines, they were in all the newspapers. (Sorry). The station hired a young announcer just a couple of years older than me, who was very funny and quite entertaining, by the name of Bob Carroll. Perfect radio name, two first names. Perhaps his parents knew something when they named him. Bob was (and still is, according to his Facebook page), a comedian, magician and ventriloquist. That summer he worked the morning show, signing the station on the air at 6:00am. But he was also working a part-time summer gig at the nearby theme park in the resort village of Lake George, about 30 minutes up the road from Saratoga.

Gaslight Village was, as you might glean from the name, a theme park based on the good ol' days of entertainment, with stage shows, ice skating shows, "meller-dramas" and the like, in and amongst roller coasters, the Tilt-a-Whirl and, well you get the picture. It was sister to one of the first theme parks in the country, Storytown, USA just down the road. That park survived and is now a Six Flags theme park now known as The Great Escape. Bob was doing his magic/ventriloquist act on stage and in the streets of Gaslight Village, evenings until about 1:00 or 2:00am. Then he would drive down the Northway (I-87) home to Saratoga, where he'd crash until his alarm would get him up at 5:30 to be at the station in time for sign-on. In theory.

Unfortunately, after a few weeks of this schedule, Bob's alarm clock was not very good at arousing the increasingly tired entertainer who was indeed, burning the candle at both ends. This eventually caused the station to NOT be be signed on at 6:00 one weekday morning. This did not go unnoticed by our boss, who set his alarm to awaken him every morning at 5:59am, so he could hear the station "starting its broadcasting day," as the sign-on announcement claimed. Mr. Jones lived just around the corner from the studios, and I was usually leaving the police station downtown around 6:00 AM, so it was a race to see who got their first to get the station started up, when Bob overslept.

After a couple of these late arrivals within a few weeks of each other, Bob was told (right there on that very same worn-out carpet in the boss's office that I was very familiar with), that next time he missed sign-on, he was history. Unfortunately, this didn't take too long to happen again, and when Bob finally ran into the studio at about 6:10am one morning, he found the boss standing there to make sure he understood he no longer worked there.

I kept in touch with Bob for a while after that, but we drifted apart until one day many years later I read in the local Albany newspaper that he's going to be appearing in a local hotel lounge trying to break the Guinness Book of World Records record for longest continuous joke-telling. I made it a point to stop in and see my old friend trying to make history by doing stand-up comedy non-stop for 24 hours, which he did! He made the Guinness Book, only to be outdone by some upstart before the next edition was published. If you want to learn more, buy his book, "The World's Most Famous Unknown Magician and Ventriloquist, Plus Tips and Tricks to Make You a Better School Show Performer." Yeah, that whole title fits on the book cover. But buy a copy soon. According to Amazon.com, there's only one copy left.

I'm not sure when I started thinking about trying to move on to a larger station perhaps within the Albany-Schenectady-Troy, NY metro market, but it was probably sometime after I'd finished my first year at WKAJ, around February of 1973. One of the things I was doing from the newsroom each morning was "stringing" for other news departments in the region. I would record phoned-in news reports of interesting stories coming out of Saratoga, for community stations serving Gloversville, Glens Falls and Troy. In turn, those news departments would send me similar reports when something of note happened in their markets.

Sometime in early spring I remember doing a report for WHAZ-AM in Troy about a gas explosion and fire at a Saratoga construction site not too far from our station. I had recordings of the police and fire chiefs explaining what happened, as I had driven much too fast in the company pie wagon (luckily, it didn't tip over) to get the story first hand. Around the same time I learned from my father that a new FM station was being built in Troy as a sister station to WHAZ, and they hoped to sign on sometime that summer. He knew this because the general manager of the station(s) had come into the car dealership where my dad worked and bought a pick-up truck to be used to get to the future transmitter site in the hills outside Albany.

Through my news contact at WHAZ, I was able to arrange an interview with the general manager, one John Linstra, to see if they were interested in hiring either a DJ or newsman for their new operation. I happened to be able to fill the bill on either count. In the back of my mind I also had the audacity to believe that once I was hired, I could convince my new boss to format the new station with rock n' roll music, a format not very prevalent on the FM dial in the market at the time. But let's not get too far ahead of the story here.

I met with John in a small room on the third floor of one of the oldest bank buildings in the United States, built back in the 1700s with brick shipped in overseas from Holland. The vault on the first floor (no longer a bank, but an insurance office) was just as old, I'm told. John's desk was in a room with several others, including a sales manager and a couple of sales people, so it wasn't a very private conversation, but he must of liked what he saw and heard because I was hired as a combo newsman/DJ for WHAZ, since the new FM station wouldn't be on the air for a while.

When I went in to give my two-week notice at WKAJ, I was met with an astonished look on Kent Jones' face. He couldn't believe I would leave such a great place to work where I seemed to like everyone and everyone liked me. He was less than pleased that I'd be taking a job within the Albany metro market for more money, like this had never happened to anyone at the station before. Most radio talent tend to take whatever steps necessary to move to bigger and better stations in bigger and better markets for more pay. That was always my plan, if you really can plan in radio.

Finally Kent accepted my notice and then said to me words I'll never forget: "You'll be back." To me, that was like waving a red flag in front of an angry bull. Instead of wishing me good luck with my still-young career in radio, he was hoping I'd fail and wind up back on his doorstep begging for a job. It made me feel all the more sure about my decision to leave and challenged me to do everything within my power to make sure I was never in a position where I'd be working for Kent Jones again.

Chapter
"14 Years" by Guns N' Roses (1991)

I do have to admit that there were times in my first few weeks on the job at WHAZ that I wondered if I'd made the right decision. I realized later in my working career that I felt this way at just about every new job I took. There are always regrets, but given time, "You can get used to anything but hanging," as my late mother-in-law was fond of saying. I quickly learned that WHAZ, owned by a Christian organization, was airing religious programming most mornings and segueing into classic country/western music in the afternoons. (The "western" part of the description was dropped as the 70s progressed and the music became more pop flavored). I was not a fan of this music at all. I just thought "twang" when someone mentioned country/western. But since I would be doing mostly news in my new position, it didn't really bother me. I didn't have to LISTEN to the station, I just had to gather, produce and read news on it. And I figured when we signed on the new, powerful FM station, now expected in the fall, we'd be programming something more palatable.

However, as with most new jobs in the radio industry, it wasn't long before I was asked to work some more hours, including Sunday mornings. On Sundays I'd play thirty-minute pre-recorded religious programs and insert news and weather breaks in between. This turned out to be more boring than playing country/western music. And depending on how late I got to bed on some Saturday nights, I'd find myself falling asleep during some of the pre-recorded programming. Only once do I remember awakening to silence, or as we call it in the business, "dead air." A big no-no. The tape had run out about two minutes before, so I wasn't out long. And the phone didn't ring, so listeners and bosses alike had not thought enough of the problem to complain.

One Sunday morning when I arrived at the station to sign it on the air at 6:00am, I noticed that one of the cart machines wasn't working. Since there were only two in the studio, this could prove to be a problem when I'd have two carted events in a row to play. I checked everything I could think of to try and fix it myself, but nothing seemed within my experience to correct the problem. I really didn't want to call Gary, our chief engineer, at a little after six on a Sunday morning. It was probably the only day of the week he got to sleep in. But, after considering my alternatives, I figured it was his main job to keep us on the air and working smoothly, so I dialed him up. I got a very tired "Hello?" when he picked up. I apologized profusely, to which he mumbled something unintelligible and said he'd be right in. He didn't live too far away. In fact when he arrived, his eyes were still at half-mast. He didn't say a thing as I rolled my chair away from the control board so he could look at the machine and figure out the problem. Within seconds he bent down, plugged the machine into an electrical outlet, stood up and wordlessly walked out of the studio.

It's obvious why this incident has stuck with me all these years. I felt like an ass. How stupid is it not to check and see if a machine has accidentally come unplugged? It's probably the first thing most people would check! I have carried this guilt with me for all these decades, and it's only just occurred to me that if Gary had asked me on the phone if I checked to see if it was plugged in, he could have probably rolled over and gone back to sleep. So I don't feel so bad anymore.

News was an important part of just about every radio station in the years before deregulation. In fact, in order for radio stations to keep their licenses to broadcast, the FCC required proof that you were serving your community in the best interest, by providing not only entertainment, but important news and public affairs programming. So as part of the WHAZ news team of about three people, I became responsible for producing a weekly hour-long public affairs interview program. Now, I don't know about you, but talking about a single subject on the radio for a whole hour, seemed like a challenge not only for the producer, but the listener as well. While I would try my best to find interesting people to talk about interesting topics, it was always a challenge.

Then I hit upon a service that would help radio news departments find interesting guests who often toured the country and went from city to city and station to station. While the topic might not always be "community oriented," we were still able to fill a whole hour with more interesting people. A couple that stick in my memory were actor George Hamilton, who was actually touting some kind of tanning product (surprise!) and the trainer of one of the most recognized felines in advertising in the 60s and 70s, Morris, the spokescat for 9Lives brand cat food.

I specifically remember that interviewing George Hamilton was terrifically easy, because as long as we talked briefly about the product he was representing, he would answer any questions I had about his life and times in Hollywood. However, interviewing the owner/trainer of a cat who did nothing but walk around while commercial cameramen tried to catch him in the act of eating 9Lives cat food, proved to be a real challenge. I believe I ran out of "interesting" questions like, "Where did you meet Morris?" and "Was that his real name when you met him?" within about 10 minutes. I wish I had that recording. On second thought, perhaps I don't.

Time seemed to drag the summer of 1973 while everyone at WHAZ awaited the OK from the FCC to start up our new station at 107.7 FM, WGNA. Some of us would be either transitioning over to the new station, or at least get additional duties on the other side of the hall, where studios were built and ready to go by mid-summer. As work progressed, transmitter testing was performed, which meant someone had to be the first voice heard on this new Albany frequency. And I got to be that person. I recorded a legal identification that simply read, "WGNA, Albany." It was played once every thirty minutes while the transmitter was on, usually in between audio tones that would test various pieces of equipment. But it wasn't long before we started getting noticed by folks who must have just been surfing up and down the radio dial in the evenings when most of the testing was done. We got a call or two from people as far away as Boston, some 180 miles to our east, as there were few other stations that high on the FM dial to interfere with our signal.

While equipment testing was progressing, management was hiring a full-time air staff made up of disk jockeys from all over the country. The morning man was local, however. Lucian J. Polverelli was late of WPTR, the 50,000 watt pop powerhouse in Albany, where he presided on the overnight shift. He used the name "Greg Lyons" on the air because they already had a jingle singing his name. To differentiate himself from previous Greg Lyons', he put the sound effect of a tiger growling between the "Greg" and "Lyons" and became popular as Greg "Tiger" Lyons. I swear, I am not making this up. This is radio, remember?

Now that I've told you all that, Jay decided to use "Jay P. Scott" as his air name on this new country music station. He would be followed by Don Murley, a mellow-voiced youngster from Scranton, PA, "Cousin" Bud Clayton, who had been working on WHAZ for a few years, "Easy" Arnie Anderson, an area native who worked full-time for New York State (from 9 to 5) on the air on WGNA from 9 to midnight, and an overnight personality from Staten Island by the name of Jim Low.

Chapter
"Fifteen" by Taylor Swift (2008)

After years of paperwork and months of planning, preparation and studio construction, "FM Country, WGNA" finally started broadcasting at 6:00pm on December 5, 1973, across the third floor hall from WHAZ. In between the two studios was the newsroom, which would now serve both stations. The first five days of music were uninterrupted by the disk jockeys as they got the feel for the equipment, and in some cases, the music. Not everyone had played country music before. Then, at 6:00 AM on Monday, December 10, 1973, regular programming began.

I pulled the morning news shift, quickly partnering with Jay P. Scott. Our personalities meshed nicely and soon we had a fun back and forth before and after newscasts that seem to catch on with the listeners. The first few months were a challenge, listener-wise, for a couple of reasons. We were competing with another well-established country/western formatted station, WOKO AM in Albany. And broadcasting in stereo FM at the top of the FM dial made it difficult for folks to accidentally find us on their radios. Plus, at the time, not a lot of cars included FM radios as standard equipment, so even new listeners could only enjoy us at home.

It took us several years and lots of free car FM converter giveaways to make a dent in the region's Arbitron radio ratings. But by the early 1980s we were in the top five, thanks to a bunch of talented broadcasters in the main studio and the newsroom. In fact, WGNA has spent the last 20 or so years as the number one station in the Albany-Schenectady-Troy, NY market, still playing country music for the masses.

Sometime in 1974 I became the news director of WGNA/WHAZ, while working the morning shift and attending mid-day and early afternoon news conferences. The hours were long, the work was challenging, and I was finally on my way to becoming the Walter Cronkite I set out to emulate. But I was not happy. I was learning that news wasn't my favorite job in radio, that I missed entertaining and ad-libbing while playing music as a disk jockey. To placate me, management granted me a weekly Saturday night jock shift, in addition to my weekday work running the newsroom. So while sounding like I knew was I was reporting on Monday thru Friday as Warren Garling, Chris Warren returned to the airwaves on Saturday nights. I knew I wasn't fooling our regular listeners by using two different names. In fact, one woman who called us regularly, called me the "Warren twins." But I very much looked forward to my six hours on Saturday nights, where I could let my strange sense of humor loose on our growing audience.

One Saturday evening I got a call on the request line from what sounded like a quite inebriated gentleman (which really wasn't a rare event for a country station on Saturday nights) asking me to play "The Yellow Rose of Texas." Now, I don't know about you, but I never thought of this song as being a country song, per se. I remember a hit version from the early 60s by Mitch Miller and his gang of singers from the hit TV show "Sing Along with Mitch," but it certainly didn't sound country to me. But this gentleman explained that he was calling from his daughter's wedding reception and they were listening to me and everyone there really wanted to hear this song.

I know what you're asking yourself: "They're playing music from a country music radio station at a wedding reception?" Believe me, I had the same question running through my head. So I, like most DJs told the guy, "I'll try to get it on for you." That was our standard answer whenever we got a request. We always wanted to sound positive and keep the listener listening, even if we knew there wasn't a chance on God's green earth that we're going to be able to fulfill the request. Many times the request is for a song you played about 20 minutes before the listener tuned in, and depending on how often the song would normally be played, it would be anywhere from a few hours to a few days before you could reasonably play the record again.

So after the gentleman hung up I just went about my business, never expecting to hear from him again. Wrong. It wasn't a half-hour later and the guy calls back, sounding even more drunk, if that's possible, and he's says he's still waiting to hear his request. I then explained to him that

I really didn't think we had the song in our library. We had been on the air a few months, but were still building our album library best we could, especially looking for records that were older and really should have in our collection. This guy wasn't giving up, though. He explained to me that he was in town for his daughter's wedding, having traveled from Miami Beach, FL especially for the occasion. He added that he was the sales manager at the Fontainebleau Hotel. He asked me if I was married, and I said I was a newlywed, in fact, having married my first wife just a few months earlier.

He then slurs to me, "If you play our shong for ush, I'll give you and your wife a free shtay at the Fontainebleau, on me." At this point I'm still not believing this guy since he sounds so wasted. All of a sudden a woman's voice comes on the line and says, "Chris, I'm his wife, and he IS what he says he is, and if he's too drunk to remember this in the morning, I'll remind him. Give me the station's mailing address." She hung up saying she hoped I could find a version and play it for them. Well now I'm intrigued, but still facing the problem that I don't remember a country version of the song. I checked through our meager library in the studio, to no avail. Then I remembered that we had a smaller library of old country albums across the hall at WHAZ. I put on a record and dashed across the hall and believe it or not, found an instrumental version of "The Yellow Rose of Texas" by Danny Davis and the Nashville Brass that was hopefully going to earn me a stay at a world-famous 4-star hotel in Miami Beach, hopefully over the next winter.

After I played the song, which really didn't belong on our playlist, the phone rang and I got an appreciative thank you and a promise that I'd get a letter from him upon his return to work in a few days. At this time in the station's history our studios were in Troy, about a 15 minute drive from the Albany post office, where we had a post office box, since our station was licensed to Albany. Morning man Jay P. Scott would drive over every morning after his shift to retrieve the mail, and I occasionally accompanied him when I had nothing better to do. About a week after my fateful request night, I started going with him daily. And every day he'd get back in the car with a pile of mail and say, "Sorry. No envelope from Florida." About two weeks later, when I was pretty sure I'd been had by a drunk loser, Jay gets in the car with the same expression on his face and starts the car to drive away. Then he smiles and hands me an envelope with the Fontainebleau Hotel logo in the return address corner. In early October of 1974 my wife and I not only stayed a week in Miami Beach, we rented a car and drove up Alligator Alley to the recently opened Epcot Center at Walt Disney World in Orlando. Unfortunately, the week we chose was a vacation week for the very generous sales manager, so we never got a chance to meet him and thank him in person.

Over the years since we shared a small dorm room in Kenmore Square in Boston, I had remained in contact with my roommate and college radio boss, Doug. He wound up working in Iowa radio, where he met a divorcee with a couple of kids and married her. He and I would mail tape-recorded letters to each other: 10" reels of tape we recorded which included our latest life experiences plus some airchecks of work we were doing on our respective stations. So Doug was acutely aware of what I could do as a broadcaster and how unsatisfied I was with my weekday newsroom duties.

In early 1975 he called me up and offered me a chance to work with him again in, of all places, Tupelo, Mississippi. He had recently relocated with his newfound family to this small southern berg about 90 minutes south of Memphis, known for being the birthplace of one Elvis Presley. You remember him, he was in all the newspapers. (Sorry. Last time, I promise). He said he'd pay me about $45 more a week if I'd come down and work as the afternoon DJ and station production director, at the small daytime AM country music station, WJLJ. He said he'd already hired the morning jock from Florida and the mid-day man from Ohio, and I would complete his new line-up.

Now, I had never lived any further south than Walden, NY, but somehow I convinced myself and my first wife that this was a good move for us. She could leave her job with the New York State University system (which HAD to pay more than I was making) and find some meaningful work 1,200 miles away in a city of 22,000 people, many of whom were still kind of pissed off about the outcome of the Civil War. Not sure what I was thinking, but with encouragement from my radio friends in Albany (a couple of whom probably wanted the job I'd be leaving), I set off in March in my

1973 white Mercury Comet with tan vinyl roof. My wife would join me with our furniture once I found an apartment in which to keep it all.

Remember earlier when I told you about second-guessing my decisions about new jobs? Usually that took a few weeks at the new position before thinking, "What was I thinking?" This time my doubts set in quite a bit sooner. Like on my drive into town after piloting my sub-compact for 17 hours. As I approached the "All-America City" of Tupelo, I drove by a couple of miles of small, rundown shacks along the side of the highway. Most didn't have any glass in their windows, but they were occupied by couples and families who sat out front in the early-spring warmth of northwestern Mississippi. It was eye-opening, to say the least. I didn't expect this in mid-20th century America.

But on the radio I was listening to that familiar Pennsylvania-raised voice of "Jay Douglas," as he described today's offerings of old chairs and mattresses up for sale on "Tradio," WJLJ's second-hand store of the air. How could this have been a bad decision? Doug helped me find an apartment in the building next to his in a modern complex about five minutes from the radio station. Of course, EVERYTHING in Tupelo was a five minute drive from the radio station. How much space can 22,000 people take up?

I quickly settled into a work routine, in my element on the air as a WJLJ "Country Gentleman." My wife found exciting sales clerk work at a local mall department store, certainly a job with an unlimited future. The general manager of the station, Charles Russell, was a young family man, maybe ten years my senior, whose wife worked in the sales office. He started out as a disk jockey and was now 49% owner and general manager of the newest of the three stations in town. The other two stations, WTUP and WELO (yes, put them together and they spell…Tupelo!), had a head start on listener numbers. But WJLJ was the only country station…until a few weeks after I arrived when WTUP decided we couldn't have all those listeners to ourselves, and started competing with us with the same format. They labeled the station "Top Dawg," and gave us a serious run for the money.

We held our own, for the most part, selling out most of our commercial time and bringing some big names of the day in country music to town for concerts: Johnny Rodruguez, Johnny Paycheck, Narvel Felts, LaCosta Tucker (Tanya's sister) and some others. Our mid-day announcer played the lead in "The Music Man" with the community theater group, giving us some closer ties with the city. It looked like we were making a real success of the signal.

After a few months on the air and in the production studio producing many new commercials a day, it was discovered that the only salesman we had out on the street offering advertising time on the station was spending quite a bit of his time away from the studio at his mistress's home. This didn't sit well with the upstanding Mr. Russell, and soon all the on-air staff found ourselves on the streets of Tupelo before and after our air shifts trying to sell ad time for our shows. I had never done this before, but I may have mentioned somewhere along the way here that you wear many different hats in small market radio, so I couldn't object when the boss put an over sized salesman's hat on my head.

I found out I was pretty good at sales for the most part. But the most important part eluded me. I found it tough to collect overdue bills from the fine folks who bought from me. After a few weeks of chasing deadbeats, I was seriously considering my next move…within the station or without it.

Chapter
"Sixteen Candles" by The Crests (1958)

In early 1976, when every man I knew decided it would be fun to grow a beard for the upcoming bicentennial of our great nation (I dubbed mine my "bicentennial bionic beard," since the Six Million Dollar man and The Bionic Woman were mainstays of popular TV at the time), my indecision about the future was moved into full gear by our boss, Charles Russell. Remember when I told you earlier that he owned 49% of the station? I did that for a reason. Turns out, his 51% partner, who owned a failing construction company, was using the station as a tax write-off, since it never made money. Since my friend and program director Doug had turned the station into a money-maker in his short months in Mississippi, he put Charles in a spot he wasn't used to. By the end of January he had fired two of the air staff (who returned home to Ohio and Florida, respectively) and put Doug and I on notice that more changes were on the way.

First, he told us we would no longer be confined to playing country music on our country music station. We could play anything our little hearts desired. He pretty much stripped Doug of his programming powers, and wrote memos daily about what we could do, say or play on the air. Doug, no slouch in the "we have a problem" department, quickly found work back in Iowa and was on his way north and a little to the left within a week or two, family and U-Haul in tow. This left me to fend for myself, working half the day on the air, and trying to figure out how to move on with my career during the other half.

I had kept in touch with some old friends back in Albany, many whom I worked with on WGNA/WHAZ. While I kept my eye on the trade publications for work on other stations in the south, I also placed a call to Jay P. Scott, still doing mornings and now acting as program director at WGNA. When he heard my sob story, he took pity on me and offered me a full-time evening air shift on the still-fledgling FM Country. Turns out his current evening air personality had separated from his wife, who had moved back to their native Philadelphia, but he spent most evenings on long-distance phone calls with her while doing his shift, and had fallen terribly behind on reimbursing the station for the cost of those toll calls (remember those days?). They were going to fire the guy and bring me back on board.

I would like to say I felt sorry for the evening jock, as I had worked with him just 11 months ago before I left Albany, but I didn't have time for that. I had bills to pay of my own and had just separated from MY wife of just two years. The plan was to get out of Dodge ASAP and head for home in my own U-Haul. Mom (who had separated from my dad just the year before — a lot of that going around) welcomed me back home, perhaps not with wide open arms, but with understanding ones.

I slipped into the evening slot seemingly seamlessly. I don't even remember getting calls asking, "What happened to the old guy?" Many listeners had long enough memories to recall me from less than a year ago doing Saturday evenings. Now they had me five nights a week and Saturday afternoons. How lucky could they be? I quickly settled into late afternoons in the production studio recording commercials and then on to the air from seven to midnight. I brought with me a couple of character voices I had introduced to Tupelo audiences (and you can see how well THAT turned out). "Clara Voyant," the soothsayer/proprietor of Clara's Café, Truck Stop and Indian Bead Emporium and her buddy "Abner Normal" or

"Abnormal" for short. They were both supposed to sound a lot older than me, because that's about the only way I could make them not sound like me. By the way, Abner got his name back in Tupelo when we held a contest to determine the best name for "The Old Prospector," which is what I originally called him.

Radio stations are always looking for new and interesting ideas for contests, rather than "The 9th called wins…" I came up with another as we approached July 4, 1976, the Bicentennial of the United States. I also brought my Bicentennial bionic beard back with me from the South, but planned on shaving it off after the Fourth of July, when all the celebrating subsided. I suggested to management that we promote that I was going to shave it off, live, on the air on July 5th, and the listener who guessed how long it would take me would win a prize.

We made a real production of it, with my friends and fellow jocks John Stanley and Eddie Dark doing play-by-play and color commentary, respectively. "And there's another long swipe down his left cheek!" And so on. The woman who came the closest with her guess won a spectacular grand prize of a 6-pack of country albums. Remember, these were the days before huge corporate entities who own the majority of today's radio stations and can afford to give away a thousand dollars an hour. The total cash value of our prize was probably about $70, but we got the albums free for radio airplay, so it didn't cost the boss anything except about 12 minutes of air time where, instead of country music, the listener heard my Norelco Triple Head electric razor and two announcers going crazy over a bionic beard hitting the floor. Classic radio stuff, but I do have pictures of this historic event in my scrapbook.

During my stint doing evenings on the radio I found myself becoming a bit detached from the real world. This was due mostly to the fact that most people meeting around the water cooler at work during the day weren't talking about what Chris Warren said on the radio last night, but rather what was happening on hit prime-time TV shows like "Charlie's Angels," "Three's Company," and the record-breaking mini-series "Roots." There was no way for me to see these most talked about pieces of entertainment, as VCRs were a rather new and expensive convenience. I didn't see Roots until it was re-aired on ABC a few years later! My regular TV viewing at the time consisted of a couple of my grandmother's favorite soap operas, as I had moved into her mobile home about a half-hour drive from the radio station.

Turns out that my mom wasn't happy with the hours I was keeping with my new job. When I finished my shift at midnight I often started my social life by meeting friends at bars and all-night diners, often getting home to crawl into bed as mom and my five younger siblings were just getting up for work or school. She didn't think I was setting a good example for my brothers and sisters. So she suggested I move in with my single grandmother, who spent summers nearby but wintered in Florida every year. She thought it would be great for the both of us, and so did my Nana. So that's how I came to enjoy the crazy story lines of "All My Children," "Days of Our Lives," and "Another World." Yes, I was a fan of Ray Liotta well before he hit the big screen, when he played Joey Perrini on "Another World." (No, I didn't remember his character's name, I just had to Google him).

One of the ways WGNA tried to set itself apart from other radio stations in our market at the time was the way we offered remote broadcasts on the weekends. During the warmer weather especially, the station was always broadcasting live from store sales and mall openings to special events throughout the region. Our FM signal was strong, so we often took our traveling radio show into small towns up to 45 minutes to an hour away. But we didn't just send one disk jockey and some free giveaways to attract our fans, we really went to town. Our appearances featured two disk jockeys standing at microphones in the middle of an old-West corral fence, along with two professional models dressed in short red skirts, white blouses and cowgirl boots, a popcorn machine offering free popcorn for the crowds, free pony rides for the kids, and free helium-filled yellow (one of our station colors, red was the other) logo-laden balloons, blown up from a brightly-painted character head that sat on top of the helium tank and looked like an old-West prospector.

While the disk jockeys handled the broadcast portion of the remote, the cowgirls popped the popcorn and handed out the balloons and other giveaways. We hired a separate company to professionally wrangle the pony rides. When our traveling road show came to a small town, the local weekly newspaper often came by to take pictures and do a story about the event we were airing from. This, of course, made the sponsors very happy as they got a lot more bang for their buck. And so did the jocks, as they were paid upwards of $100 an hour for this extra duty. In fact, it became such a moneymaker for the meagerly-paid jocks on the station that, to be fair, we had to make sure to schedule all the talent evenly, so one jock didn't make more than the other full-timers.

Another way we tried to connect regularly with our community was by playing charity slow-pitch softball games throughout the Northeast. We formed the 'GNA Country Team" consisting of full and part-time jocks, news people, sales staffers and the occasional "ringer," so we wouldn't lose EVERY game. These were contests that often drew large crowds, especially (again) in some of the smaller villages and towns who didn't have a small, local radio station. Sometimes we'd play against other radio or TV stations in the market, but often it was a firehouse team, or supporters of the charity we were there to raise money and awareness for. We featured an all-girl pitching staff as an added attraction. For quite a while (until the word got out), we would paint a grapefruit the color of the softball and toss a real fat pitch to an unsuspecting opponent, only to have the batter smash the fruit into juicy flying pieces to the joy of the crowd and other players. I usually played somewhere in the outfield where I could place my can of beer nearby on the field while I chased down fly balls. Note that I didn't say "catch" fly balls.

One of the regular benefits of playing hit records on the radio was being able to talk with and occasionally meet the top recording artists of the day. Over my years in country music I had the pleasure of interviewing some stars of note, and even introducing some on stage at their concerts. Some that you may have heard of include Dolly Parton, John Denver, Kenny Rogers, Loretta Lynn, Anne Murray, Eddie Rabbit, Ronnie Milsap, Mel Tillis, The Statler Brothers, and The Gatlin Brothers, among others. With few exceptions, these great entertainers were generous with their time and fun to interact with. They understood that their audiences and the radio professionals who played their music on the radio were important to their success.

Chapter
"Edge of **Seventeen**" by Stevie Nicks (1981)

I have quite a few great memories of the 12 (out of 13 years) that I worked at WGNA/WHAZ between 1973 and early 1986, but what you've read so far are the real highlights. During many of these years I also had the pleasure of representing the station on local TV. Whenever the local PBS station (WMHT) aired a show about country music or featuring a big country star, I would help them raise money for the non-profit by promoting paid memberships at the station during breaks in the show. This actually led to hosting evenings of their annual PBS Auction, subbing for the daily talk show host when she vacationed, and eventually a full-time position at the station in the early 2000s. Over the years I've hosted talk shows and public affairs interview shows, as well.

And for a few years one of the local network affiliates aired a semi-locally produced program five nights a week called "PM Magazine." While some of the stories were national in scope, there were two local co-hosts who would tie the stories together and occasionally invite me to help them present any stories with a country flavor. Of course, it didn't hurt that our radio station at the time resided in a 200-year-old red brick mansion that we turned into a broadcast center, complete with a video-friendly rose garden and four working fireplaces on two floors of the building in the middle of about ten acres overlooking the Albany skyline.

After one of my public TV appearances, I received a phone call the next morning that blew me away. By this time I was the program director of the station, in charge of all the on-air staff and the overall sound of the station. I was also now doing the mid-day shift, 10:00

am to 3:00 pm, which allowed me to rejoin America in front of the TV set most evenings, and occasionally "beg for dollars" as my wife calls PBS membership campaigns. Beth, our station receptionist, buzzed me in the main studio to say I had a call from Robin Allen. If you've been paying attention and remember back to the beginning of our story, Robin was my girlfriend when I first entered radio, but like most high school friends and lovers, we had lost contact a long time ago. I probably hadn't seen or spoken to her for more than 10 years. I was gob smacked (my favorite word of the week).

I picked up the phone and the first words I hear are, "You're using the NAME!" She was referring to the name she had suggested I use on the radio back in 1969, which I started using on college radio. But she had moved away from the region before I started using Chris Warren professionally in 1974. She said was visiting her family locally and she had seen me on TV the night before. She'd called the TV station this morning and asked for me and they told her I was just a volunteer there, and I worked full-time on WGNA. She shared that she and her husband of a few years, who was an engineer with Associated Press (he maintained their teletype machines) lived in New Jersey and had a couple of kids. I filled her in on my personal life, but she was still very excited that she'd had a hand in giving me my air name. Crazy.

The end of my full-time radio career was not terribly unusual for anyone who's worked on the air for more than a few weeks. The business has always been known for change, because it is, after all, a business. And to keep a business healthy and growing, change is a priority. If you get too complacent you can get left behind. I had helped get the station into the top five in the region's radio ratings, and it was successful to the point that I was able to take myself off the air to concentrate full time on keeping our air sound fresh and fun to listen to. I would occasionally sub on the air for a vacationing or sick DJ, which was easier to do than find a part-timer to come in on short notice. That's why I was completely blindsided when on January 10, 1986 I was called into the general manager's office shortly after arriving for the day. I remember the exact date because it was our son's seventh birthday.

The meeting was short, the box of my personal belongings from my office was heavy, as were the hearts of just about everyone on staff when they heard the news. I had the longest tenure of anyone working on or off the air, so depending on your point of view, my firing was overdue or never should have happened. Especially since I wasn't given any great reason for my dismissal. The boss said I had spoken out of turn in a recent newspaper interview about the station's standing in the latest ratings book. Besides being misquoted by the reporter, what I reportedly said was just common sense: ratings vary from book to book. Sometimes your competitor looks better than what they really are. Bottom line, I was out and the midday person I had hired right out of the local radio school (where I taught him a couple of years before) would take over as program director, for no extra pay. That's radio.

About six months later, after finding a job in professional services marketing (which paid a lot more than radio ever approached), one of my friends still working at the station told me WGNA was being put up for sale. Now everything made sense. What better way to improve the bottom line of the station than getting rid of one of it's top paid employees? By firing me, they could hang on to at least one-and-a-half lesser-paid employees, and still make the station more attractive to prospective buyers. I was now a bit more relieved, as no one ever wants to feel or admit they didn't do their job well. And, of course, in retrospect it's probably the best thing that ever happened to me. Getting fired opened my eyes to new possibilities beyond broadcasting and certainly professionals that paid more. After nearly 17 years since I had started in radio, I wasn't making enough to support a family of four without working a part-time job and having my wife also work at least part-time. Within five years of my firing I was earning three times what I had made in radio.

I also returned to radio part-time just a couple of years after leaving full-time work and haven't been off the radio for more than a couple of months in the last 30-plus years. I still look forward to my few hours every week that I get to put smiles on the faces of our listeners. The pocket change I bring home (yeah, the monetary rewards haven't changed much in all these years) is perfect for allowing me to have lunch with some of the many professionals I've worked with during my radio career. Two of the jocks I met as a pimply-faced 16-year-old, Paul Revere and George Washington, attend these regular lunches. We're older, grayer and heavier, but we're just as crazy as we were in our youth. Not only because we enjoyed what we did, but also because we know that it was what we were born to do.

45016175R00062

Made in the USA
Middletown, DE
12 May 2019